TAKE CHARGE
OF
YOUR
CAREER

A KIPLINGER BOOK

TAKE CHARGE OF YOUR CAREER

DANIEL MOREAU

KIPLINGER
TIMES BUSINESS

RANDOM HOUSE

**KIPLINGER
BOOKS**

Published by
The Kiplinger Washington Editors, Inc.
1729 H Street, N.W.
Washington, D.C. 20006

Library of Congress Cataloging-in-Publication Data

Moreau, Daniel, 1949-
   Take charge of your career: survive and profit from a mid-career change / Daniel Moreau.
      p. cm.
   Includes index.
   ISBN 0-8129-2829-6
   1. Career changes.   2. Mid-career.   I. Title.
HF5384.M674 1996
650.14—dc20   96-38372
                                                                                                        CIP

This publication is intended to provide guidance in regard to the subject matter covered. It is sold with the understanding that the author and publisher are not herein engaged in rendering legal, accounting, tax or other professional services. If such services are required, professional assistance should be sought.

9 8 7 6 5 4 3 2 1
First edition. Printed in the United States of America.
Book designed by S. Laird Jenkins Corp.

Acknowledgments

The notion of writing a book about careers came during a vacation on Keuka Lake in Upstate New York during one of those clear, early September afternoons for which the Finger Lakes are cherished. It was not born of personal frustration but taken from the headlines that are so common. Within a morning's drive of that idyllic scene were middle managers at Xerox, Kodak and IBM who were struggling with profound changes in their way of life. They were facing, literally, the first real setbacks of their careers, which had been spent at nearly recession-proof corporate giants with proud traditions of employment stability.

Despite its Rust Belt status, Upstate New York is no isolated example of corporate cutbacks. Cast the net wider and you find hundreds of thousands of similar case studies all across the country. It is for those people and the countless others, who, if they scramble and plan and take control of their work lives can avoid that fate, that this book was conceived.

But as it was taking shape, something more personal occurred that I believe makes *Take Charge of Your Career* even more valuable. My wife Jean became one of those middle managers who negotiated a severance from a large corporation, took vocational tests to be certain of her interests, and then launched her own business. Today, more than seven years later it thrives in a suite of offices in Columbia, Md. It has grown, too, in size and scope to offer consulting advice to developers of retirement communities across the U.S. When I began writing this book, Jean read the early chapters for advice; I showed her the later ones to be certain they were on target. Watching her successfully shift her career to build a small business inspired much of this book. It turns out it inspired me, too, and by the time this edition is published I will have made my own career shift, joining her company as director of its market study operation. I wish *me* all the best, just as I hope the advice in this book helps others making career changes.

No Kiplinger book is written without the collaborative efforts of scores of people who work diligently to ensure the accuracy, readability and attractiveness that are hall-marks of this organization. Among the people who are a part of this edition of *Take Charge of Your Career* are David Harrison, director of Kiplinger Books, and his assistant Dianne Olsufka, who carefully proofread the copy; and Karmela Lejarde, who checked all the updated and new information; the staff of *Kiplinger's Personal Finance Magazine;* and finally Jennifer Robinson for her work editing and revising this new edition.

Dr. George Joseph, M.D. provided insights and wisdom that are everywhere in this text and for those I am grateful.

This book isn't all words. We've chosen some cartoons that should add some levity and perspective to the task of career planning in the '90s.

Daniel Moreau
November 1996

Contents

Introduction

By Knight A. Kiplinger
Editor in Chief
Kiplinger's Personal Finance Magazine

Even if you are settled in your job, feeling secure about your position and not very interested in a change, the 1990s demand that you take stock of where you are and where you're heading. Too much is happening for you to be complacent. Too many companies are downsizing, slicing away at middle-management layers, getting lean as a world economy sharpens competition and makes doing-more-with-less an imperative.

No sector of the business world has been spared. Not just sick companies, but healthy companies, too, are making changes—to stay healthy. Dozens of Fortune 500 companies have slimmed down their middle-level ranks. The cuts have been deep and sustained, spilling millions of middle managers onto the street. In fact, a million fewer people, 10% of their workforce, work for the Fortune 500 companies now than worked for them five years ago.

Such fundamental changes are altering the rules for a whole generation of white-collar workers like you, many of whom will face these dilemmas for the first time in their lives. As proof, in 1993 the average tenure of displaced middle managers was six and a half years, while a decade ago it was more than 12 years.

Perhaps not surprisingly, corporate loyalty has diminished. In some cases, its demise has even been encouraged. General Electric has advised many of its employees to keep a finger on the pulse of their profession and have a resume updated and ready to use, because the decimation of middle management is not a temporary phenomenon.

Clearly, the old bond-for-life between a company and an employee has been broken.

But with change comes opportunity. And there may never have been a more promising time than today, with world markets opening and computers linking home businesses to one another and to central offices. Small- and medium-sized business, the great generator of job growth in the country, continues to thrive. Poll after poll shows a burgeoning interest in entrepreneurship.

If it's happening to you

But we're getting ahead of the story. If you're caught in a job crisis, you're unhappy where you work or you're being forced out of the company, then the immediate task is to take hold of the situation, to get control of events before they control you.

That's where this book, *Take Charge of Your Career* comes in. It's filled with information you can use now, when you're facing big decisions, to guide you through what may be the most challenging phase of your professional life. You'll also find advice on your resume, ferreting job leads from dozens of sources, turning an interview into a job offer, and negotiating that offer so that you get the best deal for you.

For those of you with a streak of independence and a willingness to take a risk, there's the huge potential of your own business. The Kiplinger organization is no stranger to that desire; this company was founded more than 70 years ago by a man with a good new idea.

And, as you read in the Acknowledgments, Dan Moreau has made his own mid-career change. After 13 years as an associate editor of *Kiplinger's Personal Finance Magazine,* he joined his wife's thriving small business as director of its market study operation. We wish him all the best in this new phase of his career.

There is a lesson you should take from this volume. Managing your career—taking charge of it—is an ongoing activity, something you do in good times as well as bad.

Knight Kiplinger

Where You Are, Where You Want To Be

Some fools get lucky and fall into a new career, no sweat. Most of us, however, have to carefully plot our way to success. Good planning takes time; it's thorough, orderly and logical. That means you do it *first*, not *as* you write resumes or go out on interviews.

Good planning requires a lot of research—up front. It's not about where the jobs are, or how to interview. It's about you and why you want to make a change. You must know why, in all its facets, before you step out of a career at mid-stage. After all, you're not a rookie with little to lose and a low price tag, but an experienced worker with a substantive record to build on, not destroy.

That's why this section is first, and why you shouldn't skip ahead to the more nuts-and-bolts portions of this book. Here you'll find answers to these nagging questions, and more:

- Is the issue you, or is it the job?
- Is it what you do, or the people you work with?
- Is it the location, size, or culture?
- Should your move be to a similar job or to another field altogether?

1

Managing Your Career

Look for a pattern in your grandfather's career and you'll likely see a man who carried his skills and interests into the marketplace and took his chances. Once he'd found what suited him, he stuck with it for the rest of his career, a welcome member of the organization, feted at the end for his loyalty.

Your father (and maybe your mother) probably followed suit, more than likely bettering granddad in the work world with a long and successful single-employer career. More retirement dinners, more gold watches, and as importantly, a fat retirement check.

The work world you live in is different. You're among the most educated people who have ever lived, many of you performing jobs that do not require the education you have received. You're accustomed to long-term planning, yet subject to more career upheaval than your parents or grandparents probably ever contemplated outside of the Great Depression and World War II. Quite probably you belong to a two-income family, but your real income has remained static for years. Despite your seemingly high income, you're spending every penny on housing, living expenses, or the cost of educating your children.

There are fewer givens in your work world than in earlier generations, and those can be chilling: Despite your training and education, your job isn't as secure as it once was. You are more transient: You'll take your skills to the highest bidder, or depending on how secure you are financially and professionally, to the company that offers you the best combination of professional challenges and personal satisfaction. And any loss of employment could easily mean you'll have to relocate to find new work. The job you find may pay less, and "cost" you more because it comes with fewer benefits.

Gerberg, Cartoonists & Writers Syndicate

As a consequence of these changes, you're likely to be more *willing* to change jobs. There's a shift from long-term corporate loyalty and a move toward greater *self-reliance*. You're in charge of a career you must manage as well as or better than you manage your department, your division—or the day-to-day flow of what you do for work. That means you're keeping up with the changes in your business, learning new skills, and safeguarding your finances against an income interruption. It means if you're smart, you're taking on more of your retirement planning than either your father or your grandfather ever had to manage. There may be a gold watch at the end of your career, but chances now are good you'll be the one buying it.

New Opportunities for You

Along with the uncertainties that accompany work life in the 1990s, there are also countless new opportunities for those willing to make the effort to take advantage of them. Not since the advent of the man in the gray flannel suit and the predominance of corporate America has there been such an opportunity for entrepreneurship—or recognition of entrepreneurial virtues.

However, chances are you're reading this book because something's wrong with your career. You want out, or perhaps more importantly, your job is threatened. You survived the first two rounds of layoffs, but that was anything but reassuring. That's particularly true when you realize that the best *predictor* of cutbacks at a company is a *history* of cutbacks. Companies that go down that road rarely turn back.

Or perhaps you've just had it with corporate life as practiced where you work. The layoffs only remind you of how poorly your company manages itself, or how chronically troubled your particular segment of the economy has become.

Maybe you like where you work, but know you need an effective plan to safeguard your job or rebuild a damaged career, or as importantly, to recognize and seize an *immediate* opportunity.

But no matter whether you're thinking about making a job change or one is being forced upon you, you know there's no trifling with your work. You have a mortgage, a child in school, car payments, a quality of life you want to protect.

Take Charge of Your Career will prepare you for the challenge of a swiftly shifting career. While changing jobs has always been a harrowing experience, in the '90s it is even more so. If you haven't been in the job market the past five or ten years, you're going to find some significant differences that affect where you will search, what you will seek and how you will find it.

Significant changes in the job market over the past five or ten years will affect where you will search, what you will seek and how you will find it.

How'd We Get Here?

Being a white-collar middle manager once brought the specter of solid achievement and, more importantly, security. It was career fulfillment for a generation of Americans who emerged from World War II, many to become the first of their families to attend college. They created middle management as America's corporations burgeoned in a postwar boom that, except for a few setbacks, continued for four decades.

But in the mid 1980s, middle management started to take it on the chin. The familiar story of blue-collar layoffs in basic industries began to hit high-tech and management people. For example, the computer industry lost ground to

It would be tough to name a Fortune 500 company that has not trimmed—some would say in most cases gutted—its ranks.

foreign competition, turning the fabled Route 128 corridor north of Boston into a land of empty office buildings and declining real estate values. That virus spread to the Silicon Valley of California, home to Apple Computer, which shed 15% of its staff worldwide by the end of 1995. IBM's story is too well known, and too depressing, to repeat, especially for the more than 100,000 people who used to work there but were asked to leave between 1986 and 1995. Mergers and takeovers led to the demise of familiar names like NCR in Dayton, Ohio and led to thousands more white-collar layoffs. Even utility companies slashed staffs in the face of declining profits. Newspapers like the *Baltimore Evening Sun* and *New York Newsday* ceased publishing, putting more managers out of work. Bank mergers that closed many branch offices cost thousands of workers their jobs.

Indeed, it would be tough to name a Fortune 500 company that has not trimmed—some would say in most cases gutted—its ranks. More than a million fewer people, 10% of that workforce, work for these companies now than worked for them just five years ago. Challenger, Gray & Christmas, a Chicago outplacement firm that tracks layoff notices, says the practice shows no sign of letting up, despite an improving economy. Too many companies are too committed to reducing what they consider bloated payrolls, to stop cutting staff. And caught in a slow growth economy with fewer options of raising prices, increasing productivity is their only hope of boosting profits. One way these employers have hoped to increase productivity is by doing more with fewer people.

In all of these shake-ups thousands upon thousands of white-collar veterans hit the streets dazed and unfamiliar with the challenges of finding a new job on short notice in a strange environment.

As if fundamental corporate change wasn't enough, peace broke out with the end of the Cold War. More than 100 military bases are scheduled to be closed in this decade. More than one and a half million defense-related jobs are expected to disappear. It will be years before some communities, devastated by the loss of a military base or a defense contractor—or both—recover. Personnel who may have anticipated a lifetime military career will not only find their plans thwarted but will have to make the leap from military into corporate culture. They'll have to define themselves in a new way, arguing their military skills have civilian applications. For them, that will mean emphasizing organization, management and teaching skills. One bright spot for some—logistics, the art and science of moving materials, something armies, navies and air forces know how to do well, is a hot skill in this decade.

There's no going back.

What makes these cutbacks different from others is a stark truth—most of the people fired from these companies or released from the military will never return. That's because they are not just victims of a recession but of basic shifts in the economy—the end of the Cold War, for instance, and by new ways of looking at how companies do business. The word of the day to describe this change in reengineering, which has at its base a simple premise: If you could redesign the company's work from the bottom up, from scratch, what would you create?

For one thing, far fewer jobs. This is a significant change in American business. Unlike earlier layoffs during recessions, when workers could anticipate being called back when times improved, these jobs are gone for good. You aren't just out of work, you're out of a career path. You aren't just looking for a new job, you may be looking for a new kind of job.

Those employees who survive cutbacks often work at whole new tasks or in organizations that perform those tasks in much different ways. And the tasks they perform today they will not necessarily perform tomorrow. Their success at staying on the job will depend on their ability to add new skills to their repertoire. This is the essence of work in the 1990s.

A stark truth: Most of the people fired from these companies or released from the military will never return.

What Happens When a Company Starts Over?

One popular manifestation has the vertically managed hierarchy, patterned after the military, replaced

"AND NOW, GEORGE, LET'S HAVE YOUR REPORT ON HOW TRIMMING THE PAYROLL HAS BOOSTED OUR EFFICIENCY AND PRODUCTIVITY!"

© 1993 Stayskal, The Tampa Tribune

with a more horizontal plan for work. Groups of employees, often called associates to reflect the blurring of ranks, join their separate skills for a given project. When they finish their task they disband. Some of them work on contract, hired as independent contractors solely for a single task or project. That's a far cry from the days of seniority, ten-year pins and award dinners.

Managers who are still on the payroll see their roles changing dramatically. First off, at many companies they no longer even manage, at least not in the traditional sense. The need to pass on commands to the lower ranks and report progress to the upper ranks, the essence of middle management's duties, has disappeared. The computer data base makes reports on progress easily accessible to anyone who cares to come on-line. No need to call a meeting, or sit through one, of middle managers giving slide shows.

Consequently, managers in many firms have become "facilitators," whose role it is to coordinate the activities of both traditional blue-collar workers on the assembly line, and highly-skilled technicians who, while they do not have management roles, are by virtue of their education, talents, skills and knowledge, powerful and independent workers. Both the empowerment of assembly-line workers and the rise of technicians can make managing tricky, even to those who realize how much the workplace has changed.

A new relationship for you

Managers aren't the only white-collar workers facing new roles. With so many of us becoming, in essence, freelance employees, corporate culture has changed. In many situations loyalty isn't just anachronistic but downright foolhardy. Consider that IBM, where employment for life was until recently a given, has let people go in droves. If IBM can do that, breaking a 50-year tradition, who can say that any company is immune? Indeed you may find some companies blessing your plans. You aren't welcome to stay on indefinitely, even when you're doing top notch work. You're just too expensive for that luxury. Today, many companies want you to think of your time on the job as project related. Project over? "Hit the road" might be too harsh a phrase, but "moving on" wouldn't be. You take your skills and experience and a good reference from the company and go find another position, which in turn will also be of relatively short-term three or four year duration. The trend is already showing up in the numbers. The average tenure of managers slipped in the mid 1990s to six and a half years. A decade ago average tenure was more than 12 years.

For those who do stay on, life is different. *Plateau* is the operative word. A lack of upward progress is the result. There just aren't enough promotions to go around. A 1989 Dartmouth College study measured the consequences. It found that workers who will be between 25 and 64 years old in the year 2000—and that covers the bulk of the work force—will have just a 34% chance of reaching a higher rank than did their fathers. In 1973, 50% had a chance of bettering Dad. The report blamed the crunch on too many middle-level baby boomers pushing against tighter corporate belts and an economy producing more line jobs than executive positions.

To acknowledge this new workplace, and yet reward good workers, companies such as General Electric and BellSouth have created programs that enrich managers' work lives but don't necessarily lead to promotions. General Electric encourages promising workers who used to "scamper" up the career ladder to broaden their skills. It's part of a plan that acknowledges, albeit informally, that the middle

For those who do stay on, life is different. Plateau is the operative word. A lack of upward progress is the result.

We are shedding our bonds to the office and the commute, redefining our relationship to the company, and fundamentally altering how we feel about the word career.

levels at GE have been squashed and good workers who want to stay and be satisfied will have to be able and willing to perform a wider variety of tasks. At BellSouth in Atlanta, a program available to managers gives them up to three years off to do whatever they want short of working for the competition. The company pays health benefits and guarantees comparable salary and job level when employees return.

The Up Side of Down

A litany of hard times and the demise of upwardly mobile corporate expectations doesn't begin to tell the story of what work will be like in this decade. Plenty of change is for the good, and will mean new and exciting opportunities for people—all kinds of people, including those whom the game might have essentially excluded even a decade ago. In a sense, few times in industrial history have offered as much opportunity for the individual as the period we're in now. We are shedding our bonds to the office and the commute, redefining our relationship to the company, and fundamentally altering how we feel about the word *career.*

Here are some of those changes:

More Americans are working at home.

Little more than a computer and a telephone connect some 16 million people to the office. That's up from 2.5 million in 1988. Still others split their work time between office and home, or use flextime schedules that let them beat traffic. Others share jobs so that they can spend more time with their families. A workforce comprised in part of part-timers, free-lancers, and flex-timers calls on new skills for workers and managers alike. Workers need self-discipline to stay on the job, good time management when they are working, and good communication skills so their managers know exactly what they've accomplished and what is left to do. Managers need good communication skills and a genuine commitment to make these alternative work plans succeed. It's no surprise these plans work best in companies with histories of innovative work programs and well-developed programs to teach communication skills and measure worker productivity. It's also no surprise that companies often make these plans available only to the best employees.

Your old boss may be your new boss.

Plenty of those homebodies are working for themselves, but their biggest client is their ex-employer. Business has discovered the value of hiring ex-employees as consultants, with some performing portions of their old jobs at a fraction of the cost. Workers get the freedom of self-employment with the steadiness of a baseline check every month. The downside is that they foot much or all of their health care costs and they live without any real job security.

You may be "temping."

Hand-in-hand with homebodies are temporary workers who report to their former employers and do the same job they did, but who actually work for another company. Temping has become a growing trend at cutting labor costs. Employers aren't responsible for pension plans, unemployment insurance, or other costly benefits. Of course, neither are the temping companies in many instances. So temporary employees work with a thinner safety net than regular employees. Still, temping is attractive to many people. For out-of-work professionals like accountants, it's a chance for employment in their field when they can't find regular work. Others stay at it because they like the change of venues that comes when they finish a project and they get to move to a new work setting—or take some time off.

It's a small world after all.

In the coming years, many of the most effective managers will have a knowledge of a second language, such as Spanish for example, and an ability to work with people from different cultures.

A foreign language skill pays off other ways, too. With many U.S. markets considered mature, companies such as

The job-hunting game for middle managers moves out of the big time to smaller firms, many with fewer than 100 employees.

Procter & Gamble, GTE and Caterpillar see some of their growth coming overseas in markets from Eastern Europe, to the Republics formed from the breakup of the Soviet Union, and from the Far East. Language skills are mandatory for many candidates who want valuable overseas experience or who will have regular contact with their company's overseas operations or customers.

Economic borders are falling with the end, or at least the beginning of the end, of trade barriers in North America and in Europe and the explosive economic growth in China. Asian- and European-owned manufacturing plants dot the American countryside. You don't have to work for the Big Three to work in the auto business in the U.S. Honda builds cars in Ohio, Toyota in Kentucky and California. BMWs will be built in South Carolina; Mercedes-Benz will be in Alabama.

America is aging.

As the average worker's age rises to 39 by the end of the decade so, too, does the opportunity for careers serving older Americans. From retailers to real estate developers, the push is on to serve this burgeoning market. That means more work for podiatrists and for people who can act as surrogates representing adult children who have moved away from their elderly parents. It means new opportunity for financial planners who can help the millions of people now in their 40s and 50s prepare for retirement.

Small is beautiful.

With so much restructuring among large corporations, the job-hunting game for middle managers moves out of the big time to smaller firms, many with fewer than 100 employees. Unlike their big corporate cousins, they will grow (they're creating half or more of all new jobs in the '90s) and need your expertise. You may miss the power of the "Rock," or whatever your old megafirm's corporate symbol was, but you also won't have to wade through all the red tape and bureaucracy of a big corporation. You may not have the pay or perks you enjoyed, but you'll have greater control over your life and maybe a chance to own a significant piece of a smaller rock.

A Course of Action

Whether these changes surprise you or not, you're probably going to be in the thick of at least some of them if you seek and find a new job. Capitalize on those changes and you are likely to find new satisfaction with your vocation, greater success in your career and a sense that you have control of events.

Right now, however, you're the holder of a rare opportunity to make anything from a minor course correction to a major restructuring. But for every promise of achievement, wealth and gain, there's a job from hell waiting to entrap another unsuspecting and eager seeker.

So you've got to do this right.

Do *what* right? That's a legitimate question for anyone to ask, especially if you're thinking of leaving (or have already left) a job because you were unhappy or if you were cut from a payroll and still feel the sting of rejection.

Chances are you'll get back on the horse and do what you've been doing. Economics dictate that you work. Your greatest assets are the skills and experience you possess now. But having adroitly negotiated a generous severance package, for example, that will give you some breathing room (as you'll read how to do in Chapter 2), or having pinpointed your source of unhappiness (Chapter 3), the

Signe, Cartoonists & Writers Syndicate

You're at a crossroads, a time to take a critical look at your record and to reconsider the career you've been in.

last thing you want to do is repeat recent history.

Consequently, you're at a crossroads, a time to take a critical look at your record. Now's the time to reconsider the career you've been in. Do you really want to move to just another company? Or should events take a sharper turn, as you start a new career? Millions of Americans do that every year. Or maybe you'll start your own business. Chances are it will be small and home-based. You're in good company because more than 14 million people already do that out of a workforce of 125 million. Chapters 5 and 6 deal with these alternatives.

No matter where your plans take you, you'll need a topnotch resume (yes, even self-employed people need resumes to borrow money from banks and to solidify new business). Your resume properly done (Chapter 7) will celebrate your achievements, not simply outline your work history. You'll learn how to sell your skills with action verbs that sing your special talents.

Digging out job leads is a big part of any job hunt. Research prospective companies (Chapter 8), and you may realize truths about your own that explain why things went the way they did. Perhaps there were talent raids before you arrived that weakened your firm, or a shift in strategy that exposed your old company to new competition. Knowing what's happened to a given company can turn you from a tepid candidate to a hot prospect as you pinpoint how you'd solve problems.

Networking is the fastest way to get a job. In Chapter 9 you learn how to make a network stronger or mend one tattered by neglect.

And what if a headhunter calls? In Chapter 10 you'll learn what to say—and what not to say—if the phone rings for you. Likewise for job interviews (Chapter 11). If you've been out of the hunt for a time, this is where you'll need the most advice. It's in the interview that the seeds of a job offer spring to life. At the same time, it's a chance for you to measure the fit between you and a job. Sure, you're looking for work, but you also want to know when a job might be wrong for you. You may find in the course of trying to sell yourself that you aren't for sale after all. The Meridian

Meringue Company will be just as well off as you if neither of you crosses paths again.

You'll need advice on tailoring an offer to fit your needs—and protect you if the job doesn't work out. You can get that in Chapter 12. Once you're on board you'll want to succeed, but that takes learning the ropes. You'll find more on fitting in to a new corporate culture in Chapter 13.

Staying the Course

Finding and getting a new position is the major step in taking charge of your career, but it is really also the first step. Staying in charge is the second and lasting move. This book will guide you through a job change, but you can use it to monitor your career in the years ahead. Plan to assess your progress periodically. Is that promotion on time? Is your salary keeping up with what others in your line of work are earning? Are you growing professionally? You may find you're ready for still more change, yet another shift in the focus of your work. You may decide that you are ready to have your own business. Or you may discover that you have made the right choice and just needed to see it outlined on paper once more. Whatever your course, you'll know it's your decision. You are in charge of your career.

This book will guide you through a job change, but you can use it to monitor your career in the years ahead.

CHAPTER

2

TWO

You're Out!

Let's suppose you picked up this book because there's a three-alarm fire raging in your career. The writing isn't on the wall, it's on a pink slip you've got crushed in your palm. There isn't time or even a need to evaluate stress or depression or whatever else that might have been ailing you. (But we'll do that in a subsequent section of this book.) You need advice, and pronto, on what to do next. For you, we'll postpone self-evaluation until the next chapter. For now, here's quick relief for your crisis.

Few people get fired anymore. They just lose their jobs. You can be *riffed, right-sized, bought out* or as they say in Great Britain, *made redundant* or any of a dozen other euphemisms for what is the bottom line: You don't go to work there anymore. But you won't get *fired* unless you really screw up, they have to call the cops to talk you down from a ledge or you're caught with fistfuls of company cash and a one-way ticket to Brazil.

A change in nomenclature doesn't make the proceedings any more pleasant, however:

Most people who've survived serious auto accidents talk about time all but standing still, of everything seeming to happen in slow motion. Tiny inane details stick in their minds.

The moment you are severed from your job may seem as searing.

"They don't hear much of what we're saying," says James Challenger, founder of Challenger, Gray & Christmas, Inc., a Chicago-based outplacement firm whose job it is to step in, at company expense, during the meeting at which the ax falls and walk middle-level employees through the process of finding a new position.

It's no wonder you need help. Losing your job is high up on the stress scale, right up there with getting a divorce, not far off from losing a child. (See pages 48–50 for an example of a stress test. You may want to take it to see just how you rate.) Even if you saw it coming or you had nothing to blame yourself for, the scars can be deep and lasting, the sense of bitterness and betrayal all too real. The financial loss can be staggering and long term for some.

No one working in this decade should underestimate the risks of the 1990s and the end of the job security that many middle-aged, middle-level managers have come to expect in return for their loyalty.

Steiner, Cartoonists & Writers Syndicate

In the Immediate Aftermath

The short advice for those facing involuntary termination is to keep your head about you. Yes, you're being cut from the payroll, but chances are you aren't out of the door, or off of the books, yet. You may still have power to negotiate a host of benefits that will help you through this stressful time, chief among them time itself. Time when you'll be at the phone number listed on your business cards, time when you'll still, at least technically, be what the title on your door says you are.

Just as you negotiated your way into a company (see Chapter 12 for more information on that), you are going to negotiate your way out of one. Depending on your position and the company you worked for, as well as the circumstances of your departure (a merger makes for a different

Keep your head about you. You may still have power to negotiate a host of benefits that will help you through this stressful time, chief among them time itself.

situation than a downsizing, for example), you may have some work ahead of you. Your salary probably wasn't the only thing you drew from the company coffers.

- **You could have been given tuition guarantees for your kids.**

- **You may have sales commissions or performance incentives** on deals already completed that you are entitled to receive.

- **Don't overlook vacation or other compensatory time** to be included in your settlement.

- **There's your pension, profit-sharing or other retirement plans** you were in that need to be paid out to you and properly rolled over into new accounts. Do it incorrectly, and you could be penalized by the IRS.

- **Even the date of your departure from the payroll** can be negotiated. Staying on board through a certain date could make you eligible for a prorated or year-end profit sharing distribution, for example.

- **In most instances, your health benefits can and must be transferred to interim programs if you choose.** But go shopping for other insurance; while any individual health insurance policy can be expensive, possibly costing several hundred dollars per month, you may find something cheaper than what your company is offering.

As you'll learn later in this chapter, you have some leverage. Your company has something on the line too—its reputation inside and outside the building. Other employees are watching what you get and how you got it. Morale during a layoff or merger is already lowered. Messing with departing employees sends nothing but a bad message to those who remain.

On a more personal and emotional level, there's the risk a disgruntled employee will decide that frontier justice is called for. No boss ever fired anyone without thinking of that. It's another reason to handle these negotiations with great care.

For you, beyond controlling the emotional chaos, there is the challenge of a fiscal world turned upside down. As your income falls, your spending also will probably have to be cut. It may take you up to a year to find another position. For most people, that much absence from a full-time payroll check will mean big changes in the way they live.

Your psyche will take a battering as well and you may need therapy to deal with the stress, anxiety and depression. You may feel the stages of mourning—denial, anger, depression, acceptance.

Or, surprisingly, you may find the process almost exhilarating. You're free at last of a job you detested. Getting laid off might be the catalyst for a new career, your own business or a chance to return to school. (More about that in Chapters 4 and 5.) For older executives, a study by Right Associates, a Philadelphia-based outplacement firm, says that new careers may make the most sense. The study revealed that while 55% of those under age 50 changed industries, 63% of the 50–59 year-olds switched and fully 78% of those over age 60 found jobs in new fields. True, the study acknowledges, much of this reflects the difficulties older workers face in finding jobs equivalent to what they have lost. But it can also represent a chance for a new course and a rejuvenated worker. In this decade that situation may ease as companies stretch retirement age to hang on to skilled and experienced workers.

Surprisingly, you may find the process almost exhilarating.

A temporary solution

A break in steady employment may mean you take temporary work. According to John Thompson, founder of Interim Management in New York City, part-time work is a way to literally buy some time. Executives who took half-day assignments, for example, kept money flowing into their coffers. That took at least some of the heat off their finances. And with a role that can accurately be defined with the word consultant, part-time work can also soothe a bruised ego. There's an office to go to but still the time to continue a job search—without feeling a desperate pressure to find something fast. Temping is also a valuable source of job leads. Many companies use temping to screen prospective employees—and vice versa. But as you'll learn later, this is not a time to loaf. Temporary work should be just that—*temporary*—until your job search pays off with a full-time offer.

For an inside look at temping, read *The Temp Track*, by Peggy O'Connell Justice (Peterson's). Justice has 20 years of temping experience at law firms, teaching hospitals, hotels and publishing houses.

Separation Anxiety

You can't be expected to be privy to every inside decision where you work. You can't know about every takeover plan being hatched at a rival company. You aren't responsible for the legislation that came out of Washington that means your company's way of doing business is going to change. You've got enough responsibility on your hands with your own work. Head down, you say, shoulder to the wheel, eyes on the road. (The punch line, of course, is now try to work in that position!)

Too often we are blindsided by events beyond our control. That's what happened to Henry Ryan, once an executive with the Gulf Oil Corp. in Pittsburgh, Pa. When he joined the company at age 37 as a director of human resources, he said he expected that would be his last employer, that he would retire from the firm and collect a handsome pension one day. Gulf might have wished the same for him, but Chevron Oil Corp. had other plans. In 1984 it completed a takeover of Gulf Oil that ended the firm's tenure as a bulwark of Pittsburgh industry. For Ryan and nearly every other executive at Gulf it meant an offer of a new job. In and of itself that was a kind gesture. Many mergers or attempted mergers lead swiftly to layoffs as companies slice away redundant or weak divisions.

But from there, Ryan began to lose control of his career. Chevron was offering him a lateral move at best in salary terms and a questionable one in terms of his responsibilities. While he quickly pointed out that the company found a similar lateral position for his wife, also a Gulf employee, the move was taking them from Pittsburgh to San Francisco. His $86,000 Pittsburgh home, not far from his job, cost more than $200,000 to duplicate—and that was in Oakland, which, because of traffic, was a long and arduous commute. Chevron's culture caused him other problems we'll discuss in Chapter 13.

He lasted a year before returning to Pittsburgh to a human resources position with the Duquesne Light Co., a public utility company. Not too long after, he moved to a similar position with a utility company in New Orleans. Ryan admits his plans do not include retiring from the utility, but he plans to finish out his career in a corporate environment.

"What it pointed out to me is the uncertainty of life. That really changed me," he says ruefully. You'll find his story repeated thousands of times at places like Westinghouse, Lockheed Martin (formerly Martin Marietta), or Raytheon—companies that depended on defense contracts to keep their payrolls high. Or to places like General Electric, Procter & Gamble or Scott Paper, companies dedicated to doing more with fewer employees. Or Digital and IBM, companies with long-standing no-layoff policies that fell victim in the 1990s to hard times. For almost 40,000 AT&T employees, the abrupt end of their careers there came on the heels of a breakup of the company into three parts in 1996.

The Boss Wants to See You

It's not often you'll be pink-slipped out of a job in a swift move at the end of the day. As we noted, times warrant a more calculated approach from management, if not out of consideration for the departing employee, at least to avoid legal and other entanglements. Instead, you'll probably be ushered into a meeting in some neutral place with your supervisor, a secretary to record the event and perhaps a representative from an outplacement firm hired by your company to help you through the experience.

In what will undoubtedly be a carefully scripted procedure designed to cover all the bases and let you down as gently, but firmly, as possible, you'll be told of your termina-

Ideally, the meeting will last less than 15 minutes, you won't have created a scene and you won't have to face your colleagues until you are ready.

tion, probably given some specific reasons for it and offered a severance package of benefits which can range from added salary payments to health benefits and the aforementioned outplacement help. The package will be similar to those given anyone with your responsibilities and experience. It will probably err on the side of generosity, as much because that's an excellent public relations tool for those who remain as it is the action of a thoughtful company taking care of its own.

If the meeting is ideal, it will last less than 15 minutes, you will not have created a scene and the boss will make some arrangements for you to exit the building without having to face your colleagues until *you* are ready.

In most cases your boss won't be enjoying the experience much more than you are and will be sympathetic to your plight. However, in most cases this is not a time when arguing against this course of action will have any merit. You are being laid off, not offered a second chance at your job.

If you're good on your feet (or in this case, in your seat), or not especially upset by what is happening, you can start negotiating for more severance benefits if you think you deserve them. But in the spirit of getting this dirty little job over with, you can ask to meet again to discuss your severance. That gives you time to gather your wits.

Depending on the situation, you may be forced to clear your desk immediately. This happens most often where classified work is being conducted for the U.S. government or where you are involved in research and development. Adding to the humiliation, a security guard may watch over you and inspect everything you

DILBERT reprinted by permission of United Feature Syndicate, Inc.

are taking from the building. But it is more probable that you'll be given time to make an exit, even up to a month or more. Don't let pride stand between you and that opportunity. Your business phone and office—and your title, however hollow now—are valuable and are the tools of trading jobs.

Give Yourself a Break

In the short term, give yourself some breathing room. Take two or three days off. Don't call about jobs, don't fire off a packet of resumes to every want ad in the newspaper. You won't be at your best in this period, so it's foolish to be trampling your best contacts now. Let your head clear. If you're concerned about your mental health, consider seeing a doctor or a psychiatrist. To help deal with the stress, get plenty of sleep and exercise but stay on a normal sleep schedule. Sleeping through the day as an escape (and consequently not being able to sleep at night) will take its toll on your health, your family life, and your ability to formulate a plan and execute it.

As you settle down you'll be in a better position to devise a game plan *into* a new job instead of conjuring the point in the day when blowing up the company headquarters would be most effective. You'll also be better able to determine if your termination was fair.

Don't leave your family out—and don't even think about not telling them. At best, traipsing off every morning as if you were going to work is pathetic. At the worst, it's deceitful and insulting to the people who care about you the most. And it denies you the most immediate support available to you at a time when you may already feel isolated and lonely. Why make it worse?

Sharing this time with your family helps you set events in context. Unemployment is not a terminal disease. You need to make it plain to your family, if they don't already sense it, that while this is a big event for all of you, it's something that can happen to people who work. You and your family will get through it, just as you would any other life event you share.

Don't deny yourself the support of those who love you at a time when you may already feel isolated and lonely.

Compare the cost of continued health coverage through your company with that of private health insurance, which might be cheaper.

A Fair Severance Package

While you're taking a few days off to adjust to the news, consider the terms of your severance. You were probably given a letter spelling it all out. If you didn't get one, call and ask for one. Your company might have a strict formula it adheres to with regard to these benefits, but there is often room for improvements to be made.

To help guide your own deliberations, here's what's considered a reasonable benefits package by outplacement firms. You should be able to receive much of this if you are laid off. Your specific severance will probably vary according to the industry you are in, your employer's practices and your rank and time with the company.

A month's pay for every year you've worked there

Lower-level or shorter-term employees can expect three to six months of pay. Mergers may result in more months of pay. Generally, it's better for you to take the payout in monthly installments if you can get them. You're more likely to continue to be eligible for company-paid health benefits if you are still on the payroll. It helps keep your spending on a steady course if the money comes in as it always has.

There are exceptions where a lump sum is a better idea. If you are near retirement it may make more sense to receive the entire severance amount in a lump sum you can add to your own benefits package. If you are considering going into business for yourself, it may make sense to receive your pay up front to help you get started.

Health and life insurance

No matter how your payout is given you, you can negotiate for continuation of benefits such as health and life insurance, for a specified term. You can negotiate for coverage until you find another job, and if possible, throughout the waiting period before you're actually covered by your new employer's insurance plan. If you work for a company with 20 or more employees that has a health plan you must be offered continued health coverage under COBRA. You'll pay what the company paid plus up to 2% and you can be covered for a period up to 18 months. Don't overlook this important benefit, especially if you or someone in your family has a pre-existing condition that would make it hard to obtain health insurance. But compare rates with private health insurance. You may discover you can get cheaper coverage from another source. Start with Blue Cross and Blue Shield in your state. It often has the least expensive rates for short-term coverage. If you're married and your spouse is covered by a separate health insurance plan, find out whether you could sign on as a dependent. This is often the least expensive option. But, whatever your choice, be sure to use your company-supplied coverage as a bridge if there is a waiting period (generally three months) when you will not be covered by new insurance policies.

If you don't require outplacement help, you can ask for more cash.

Agreement on the wording and the timing of the announcement of your exit

Your reputation and your image in the job market are at stake. This is likely to be your last chance to control how your soon-to-be former employer will be characterizing your tenure with the firm. This may be less of an issue if you're being laid off with a cast of thousands, but if you're one of the first or the only one to go, or if you've been fired, you'll want to conduct your own damage control.

A promise of a decent reference

You should ask for a written letter of reference you can use in your job hunt. If your employer valued you and is letting you go through no fault of your own, you can probably expect all the praise that you're due. If you and your employer are mutually agreed that you should go, or at least are still on speaking terms, you can try to work out the wording of a reference before you leave. That will help avoid the silence or the carefully worded but essentially meaningless statement some employers give out that is little more than a veiled message that you were trouble. If you left under the worst circumstances, the best you can hope for is that your former employer won't say anything at all;

Have your retirement funds transferred directly to a new IRA to avoid having 20% withheld as credit against federal income taxes.

laws regarding what an employer can say about you without risking a slander or libel suit will limit criticism for many.

Outplacement assistance

If you're a higher-ranking member of the company, or part of a larger exodus, you may receive outplacement service paid for by your company as a matter of course. If not, ask for it. Outplacement services are not employment agencies; they don't find job leads for you. Instead, they coach you through the personal stress and professional loss you are experiencing, to help polish your resume and interview skills and even supply you with a phone, secretarial help and office space from which to work. Some companies have their own in-house outplacement services. The NCR Corp., in Dayton, Ohio, for example, offers training in job-hunting skills for workers losing their jobs. Karl Stein, an engineer for a decade with the company, recently took advantage of the training to get advice on starting his own business. If you don't need outplacement—you have another job lined up or you're starting a business—you can ask for more cash.

Reimbursement for some of your job-hunting costs

Costs such as office rental, a phone, car expenses and clerical help are often paid as part of a severance package. You may receive money to pay for education or training for a new vocation. Some companies are generous enough to offer assistance to a spouse, just as they did during the initial relocation.

Help in returning home

Suppose you relocated for this company and then got cut loose. There you are in Minot, desperately missing Miami. You may find your company willing to pay for your move back. You can argue that job hunting in or from North Dakota is more difficult than working out of a home port, a place where you have a network. Largesse like this often lessens the desire to litigate. Your company probably appreciates this fact more than you do.

Payout of retirement funds

You may have retirement investment packages—a 401(k), for example, or a profit-sharing plan earmarked for your retirement. Don't neglect to arrange for the payout of these plans in a timely manner, and as we noted earlier, it's best in most circumstances for you to have your employer make the transfer. To avoid having 20% withheld as credit against federal income taxes, have your retirement funds transferred directly to a new IRA. You can deposit it into a money market fund at first, then reinvest the money after you develop a financial plan.

It's important to keep your hands off the cash, and not just because of the temptation of a lump sum of money. The tax bite kicks in if you take possession of the money. A financial planner or your former company's benefits office can help you with the paper work. If you owe on a loan against your 401(k) plan or other profit-sharing plan, the balance is generally due when you leave the company. Be sure the right amount is deducted from your payout when you leave by checking your record of payments (another reason to hang onto pay stubs).

Play It Like a Pro

Approach your negotiations as a piece of business you are conducting with your firm. As best you can, resist making it personal. The best negotiations leave both sides feeling that there was give and take. Besides, all of you will probably live to do business again, most likely with one another. There's no sense in burning any bridge, no matter how angry you may be at the moment.

Virginia Lord, a former vice president of Right Associates, says many people find it hard to properly evaluate the severance they are offered. Bearing in mind who pays for outplacement, you can ask a counselor to help evaluate yours. You may be shown national averages for your position or trends in what is offered by companies like yours. You can talk with others being severed to compare your settlement with theirs. An attorney who specializes in labor contracts or your accountant can also help you mea-

If you fight, you're going to be fighting for a long time, and even if you win, you could lose in the job marketplace.

sure the size of the package. Your local bar association can help you find an attorney.

Legal Redress

Some people aren't surprised when the ax falls. They were privy to the company's books and knew something had to give. Or they saw their division sliding into corporate oblivion, the stepchild of the firm. When it didn't sell, it had to be closed.

For others, the decision is jarring, the terms harsh. You're steamed at the injustice of what's been handed you: "Why wasn't there another place for me in this bloated bureaucracy?" you demand. Wait until a jury hears this one. If

Bill Hughes: Choosing a Buyout Offer

Looking at a buyout offer is clearly better than staring at a layoff notice. But as Bill Hughes, a network designer for SNET, Inc., (Southern New England Telephone) learned, it carries special challenges.

In exchange for ending a 30-year career with the phone company, Hughes, then 48, was offered seven options. Each involved sweetened benefits—almost invariably the key to a buyout offer—and it was up to Hughes to figure out which one was best.

His choices included: a single-life annuity that would pay him nearly $2,000 a month for life, starting immediately.

There was a joint-and-survivor annuity that would pay him about $1,750 a month for life; his wife would receive $872 a month if she survived him.

He was also offered a "lump sum certain" option that would pay him $1,900 a month for life. If he died before collecting a total of $275,000, his wife would get the remainder of the lump sum.

Or he could take a lump sum of $275,000 in cash and roll it into an IRA.

On its face, the choices were daunting. But since the cost to the company is about the same in each case, there is really only one decision to make: does he want the guaranteed income of an annuity or the potential for more money from investing a lump sum?

Hughes opted for the lump sum after figuring it would grow to more than $775,000 by the time he reached age 60, assuming a 9% annual return. That's enough to provide about $7,250 a month in 1996 dollars over his 18-year life expectancy at that time.

"When I considered that the annuity was fixed, and how devastating even 4% annual inflation can be, the lump sum made more sense," Hughes says, because it can outpace inflation.

His hoped-for 9% return is within historic parameters of the stock market, whose returns have averaged more than 10% annually since 1926.

you're part of upper management your feathers may be ruffled by how you were valued or the manner in which you will be paid off. Serious money is involved. Cooler heads are not prevailing.

For you, a juncture looms. If you accept the separation terms, you may be bitter for a long time. If you fight, you're going to be fighting for a long time, and even if you win, you could lose in the job marketplace. Suing your boss, or the company that let you go, is no light matter. You can't bank on using it as a tactic to show them how seriously upset you are without weighing the ramifications if the company decides to call your bluff—and plenty have, even when it was a stupid idea in the end.

Still, if you have been wronged, you should be compensated. Plenty of people have been. A big corporation facing off against a little person like you knows full well on whose side a jury of your peers is likely to be. According to Jury Verdict Research in Horsham, Pa., a survey of more than 500 wrongful dismissal trial verdicts between 1988 and 1995 showed that age bias cases where the plaintiff won yielded the biggest settlements, averaging $219,000. Sex discrimination cases settled for an average of $106,728; race bias claims settled for $147,799 and disability claims settled for $100,345.

There are some caveats to these findings. They represent, after all, only the winners in *jury* trials. So they must be weighed against the more analytical leanings of a judge in the case and of the appeal process. You should know, if you didn't already appreciate it, how entangling a lawsuit can be. No one is kidding when they say it can span years, a chronic headache always present in the back of your head.

It will help you to understand the status you have as an employee if, before you load any figurative guns for battle, you consider how you held your job in the first place. Yours could be a more tenuous link than you realize, depending in which state you live and how you were hired and treated on the job. The root of all this is an archaic term you may one day wish had a strictly military rather than a vocational meaning.

At least 30 states have ruled the promises in employee handbooks are enforceable as implied contracts even when they include statements to the contrary.

Fire at Will

Most companies have gotten good at creating a paper trail that leads an employee right out the door.

Time was most everyone worked under the concept of "at will," which had its roots in the master-and-servant relationship of Roman times. Unless you had an employment contract that stipulated otherwise, if your boss didn't like you, you were gone. Much of the argument came from the obverse. You had that right, why shouldn't the boss?

That's still the case for many, many employees. But the concept is coming under attack from a number of fronts and in a series of court cases. Many people are covered by civil service protection, antibias laws, and individual and union contracts that make their dismissal less easily accomplished. Until recently, the courts protected employers of the rest with a narrow view that the court's role was limited to deciding whether an employee contract existed. If it did not, according to the courts, an employer was free to fire at will.

First came anti-discriminatory laws aimed at terminations based on race, sex, marital status, age, religion, national origin and handicaps. (If you suspect any of the above factors led to your dismissal, contact the Equal Employment Opportunity Commission for help. You can find local offices listed under the U.S. Government section in your telephone directory.) Then came court challenges to the notion of "at will" employment and judges began to interpret the laws to say that "at will" as a reason to fire someone was illegal.

The arguments stems from four sources. First, the thinking goes, your job is property in a constitutional sense and under the 14th Amendment of the U.S. Constitution, you can't be denied your property without due process. Of the arguments, that is the least common one used. Of more value to the judges in the states that have applied exceptions to the "at will" doctrine, are these.

Implied contract

Even though one may not literally exist, a contract between the employer and employee may indeed be in effect in the language of an employee handbook or in remarks made by a boss about the employee's future with the company. Courts have ruled those statements imply a contract. But in the time since these cases were argued, companies have modified employment handbooks to thwart the argument that the handbooks are contracts. Nevertheless, at least 30 states have ruled the promises in these handbooks are enforceable even when they include statements to the contrary. Keep a dated copy of the employee handbook in effect when you were hired and any updated copies. If you work under a contract, keep a copy of that with your most important records. If you have access to your personnel records, get copies of those, including performance reviews and your pay history. Show any of these materials that you have to your attorney along with anything you received in writing at the time you were notified of your termination.

"You didn't fool me for one minute! You're not a Kelly Girl. You're Dimpleman -- the guy I fired last week!"

Schwadron, Cartoonists & Writers Syndicate

The principle of good faith and fair dealing

Despite the doctrine of "at will," an employer has a moral obligation to deal with an employee fairly and in good faith. As a result, a capricious or malicious dismissal could be a cause for legal action. But as a result, employers today understand they must buttress their terminations with written evidence of cause and their attempts to remedy the problem short of your dismissal. Most companies have gotten good at creating a paper trail that leads an employee right out the door.

The mark on your career as someone who sues when you get in a bind outweighs almost anything you could expect to accomplish in court.

A concern for public policy

Here the greater good of society applies. You can't be fired for serving on jury duty or for filing a worker's compensation claim.

The Legal Reality

While these arguments have led to justice for some who were wronged, don't kid yourself into believing the courts are a course to follow after you're fired. Your chances of winning there are slim even in the 38 states considered to be sympathetic to employees by virtue of the statutes on their books and the decisions in their courts. (The pro-boss states are Alabama, Delaware, Florida, Georgia, Indiana, Louisiana, Mississippi, New York, North Carolina, Ohio, Pennsylvania and Rhode Island.) Most judges side with the employer in all but the most blatant abuses.

Supreme Court decisions in the late 1980s strengthened management's side of the argument. In *Wards Cove Packing Co. v. Atonio,* a 1989 case, the Court said the plaintiff bears the burden of disproving a company's assertion it was acting neutrally. That overturns a ruling in 1971 where the Court said discrimination was proved even if a practice was fair in form but discriminatory in action.

A second 1989 decision, *Martin v. Wilks,* the Court ruled that whites affected by a court-ordered affirmative action plan could sue to reopen the case. The former ruling said the rights of whites were not violated in such cases. In a third 1989 decision, *Price Waterhouse, Petitioner v. Ann B. Hopkins, Respondent,* the court did shift to protect the defendant, but the ruling was for cases where discrimination was a factor in dismissal. The Court said the burden of proof could shift to the defendant in discrimination litigation.

The 1991 Civil Rights Act evened up the sides when it restored some workers' rights to sue for job discrimination, according to attorney John Rapoport, a New York attorney who specializes in employment issues. He says employees were already seeing the fruits of other changes in the system. "There's a much better climate for plaintiffs," he explains. "There is now an increased awareness among judges on all levels and an increased understanding among juries. If you walk into a courthouse, you find both judges and juries more willing to grant bigger judgments."

In 1996, the Supreme Court decided that age discrimination is age discrimination, even if you're being replaced by someone over 40. The Court ruled that workers age 40 and over can sue employers for age discrimination even when the workers who replace them are also 40 years of age or older.

Lower courts had ruled in some cases that older workers were barred from bringing suit if they were replaced by someone also protected by age discrimination laws.

At the same time, employers are also more savvy. "You don't see memos anymore that say, 'get rid of the old guy,'" he explains. "So the vast majority of cases are settled on 'pretext.'" You can define pretext as "you are doing well, then you are fired and someone younger and cheaper is hired and you are told you had lost your skills. Companies know that is a reason they can fire you." Enter the aforementioned savvy jury. "Juries know how to judge performance," says Rapoport.

The Practical Reality

Even if you are comforted by the notion of smarter juries and consider a lengthy legal action worth the effort, the truth is, unless you are starting your own business or nearing retirement with few prospects of finding another job and so have little to lose, the mark on your career as someone who sues when you get in a bind outweighs almost anything you could expect to accomplish in court. And you almost certainly won't get your job back, assuming you even want it. Still, filing a suit can move stalled negotiations, proof being that no more than 5% of all suits filed go to trial.

If you are considering legal action, talk to an attorney. Do it within a week or two of your severance when your memory is sharp, and the principals are all still in place and could produce physical evidence like memos and company statements.

You can locate lawyers who specialize in labor law or employee rights in the Yellow Pages or through your local

Track your expenses, dollar by dollar. Also, look at your assets as if they are in layers, ordered according to their liquidity.

bar association, which will refer you to attorneys. An initial visit under this arrangement generally costs under $25. Lawyers work on an hourly basis or on what is called contingency where they collect a portion of any settlement, generally about one third of the money awarded. The latter is cheaper for you, but you'll have to have a stronger case, with more at stake, to attract a lawyer willing to take your case on contingency. Even then, you may have to front some money for expenses.

If you are a member of a professional association, it may be able to help you with staff legal advice or a referral to a lawyer in private practice.

Even if you don't end up in court, an attorney can advise you on tactics and evaluate your severance package and any counteroffers you receive if you go through several rounds of bargaining. You'll pay the attorney's hourly rate for these services. Manage his or her time carefully, bearing in mind that even phone calls you make to check on how things are going will undoubtedly turn up as time charged to you.

A Plan for Your Money

You may have worked only eight hours a day, but your job fueled most of what you did the rest of the time. Lose it and besides finding another one, you've got mouths to feed, a mortgage payment and a car sitting in the driveway that won't go anywhere without gas. It is for this time that financial advisors told you to salt away at least six months of living expenses. It ought to be twice that, according to Harry Millios, a former partner in Santos and Postals, a Rockville, Md., accounting firm. The reasoning is simple: It can take nine months to a year to find another position.

Millios has walked more than a few clients through periods of unemployment. The process begins with filling out a personal financial statement. You should do one each year, anyway, particularly if you have investment real estate holdings, stocks and bonds and other assets with variable values. The task is to determine your net worth, the difference between your assets and your liabilities. Obviously, the former is supposed to be larger than the latter. The goal while you're unemployed is to keep it that way.

That's the goal. Reality may intrude, you may have to tap your assets, you may have to raid them in fact to keep your house, to pay taxes, to feed the kids. So be it. Assets can be used for that, too. But not all assets are equal. Not all bills are due on the same day. So you'll need strategy and tactics to get you through this dent in your cash flow. Use the worksheets on pages 36 and 37 to track your monthly cash flow and to assess the assets and debts that add up to your net worth.

Putting on the Brakes

Losing a paycheck means different things to different people. If you're wealthy, the wolf won't be at the door anytime soon. If you're the sole support of six children, you have a different agenda. If you are like so many people, half of a two-income household, you're somewhere in the middle.

Maybe your spouse can cover the mortgage and groceries, but you'll have to juggle any other expenses. If you weren't already a careful spender, you'll need to be now. For all our optimism that you'll find another job quickly, there is no guarantee you won't have to tighten your belt first. If you're like most people, you probably haven't been keeping close track of how you've been spending your money. Start keeping track of it now, dime by dime (dollar by dollar will be close enough). Hang on to every scrap of paper related to your spending. You

"I figure if they do fire me, they'll have to pay me a week extra until I clean my office."

From The Wall Street Journal, Permission, Cartoon Features Syndicate

can even carry a little notebook to have a record of your spending. Between that, your checkbook, credit card slips, and receipts from stores, cleaners, restaurants, etc., plus some soul searching should get you close enough.

Continued on page 38

Your Cash Flow

Income	Total for Year	Monthly Average
Take-home Pay	$ _____	$ _____
Dividends, Capital Gains, Interest	_____	_____
Bonuses	_____	_____
Other	_____	_____
Total Income	$ _____	$ _____

Expenditures		
Mortgage or Rent	$ _____	$ _____
Taxes not withheld	_____	_____
Food	_____	_____
Utilities and Fuel	_____	_____
Insurance Premiums	_____	_____
Household Maintenance	_____	_____
Auto (gas, oil, maintenance, repairs)	_____	_____
Other Transportation	_____	_____
Loans	_____	_____
Medical Bills not covered by insurance	_____	_____
Clothing Purchases and Care	_____	_____
Savings and Investments	_____	_____
Charity	_____	_____
Recreation and Entertainment	_____	_____
Miscellaneous	_____	_____
Total Expenditures	$ _____	$ _____

Summary		
Total Income	$ _____	$ _____
Minus Total Expenditures	_____	_____
Surplus (+) or Deficit (−)	$ _____	$ _____

How to Figure Your Net Worth

WHAT YOU OWN

	$ Amount
Cash	
Cash on hand	_____
Checking accounts	_____
Savings accounts	_____
Money-market accounts	_____
Life insurance cash value	_____
Money owed you	_____
Marketable Securities	
Stocks	_____
Bonds	_____
Government securities	_____
Mutual funds	_____
Other investments	_____
Personal Property (Resale Value)	
Automobiles	_____
Household furnishings	_____
Art, antiques and other	
collectibles	_____
Clothing, furs	_____
Jewelry	_____
Recreation and hobby	
equipment	_____
Other possessions	_____
Real Estate (Appraised Value)	
Homes	_____
Other properties	_____
Retirement Funds	
Vested portion of	
company plans	_____
Vested benefits	_____
IRA or Keogh plans	_____
Annuities (surrender value)	_____
Other Assets	
Equity in business	_____
Partnership interests	_____
Total Assets	$_____

WHAT YOU OWE

	$ Amount
Current Bills	
Rent	_____
Utilities	_____
Charge-account balances	_____
Credit card balances	_____
Insurance premiums	_____
Alimony or child support	_____
Other bills	_____
Taxes	
Federal	_____
State	_____
Local	_____
Taxes on investments	_____
Other	_____
Mortgages	
Homes	_____
Home equity	_____
Other properties	_____
Debts to Individuals	_____
Loans	
Auto	
Education	_____
Other	_____
Total Liabilities	$_____
Total Assets	$_____
Minus Total Liabilities	–_____
Your Net Worth	$_____

Arrange with your creditors to reduce your monthly payments— even possibly your mortgage—for a set period of time.

As for now, most of the dinners, the vacations and the new "toys" are on hold. (Think of the celebration you'll have when you get another job.) You'll need to manage your money more carefully than ever. You may feel shame. Spare yourself, nearly everyone comes out of the other end of this time saying the experience gave them insights on their spending habits and convinced them to budget more carefully after the crisis was over.

Don't borrow just to keep up appearances. Involve your family, rather than hiding your ups and downs from them. Your feelings will show anyway, and you may find you are drawn more closely together. You may also find displaced anger showering itself on your family and friends. Recognize it when it appears and try to control it. If you need psychological help, don't hesitate to get it. Carrying that anger into the job hunt can seriously cripple your chances in many instances.

Work/Family Directions, a Boston-based consulting firm, offers workshops to families of its corporate clients. Seminar director Alice Freedman tells parents to assure their children that while things are not *fine*, they will have what they need. Parents should tell children, however, that their spending habits will change and they will have to be careful with their money. Freedman says it may help to tell teachers, friends and caregivers about the situation so they can offer support to your children.

Surviving the Crash

Many automobiles today are constructed to collapse in segments, grill to fenders, fenders to hood and so forth. The purpose is to protect you inside the car by having the segments absorb as much of the impact as possible.

Your financial plan while you are unemployed should be constructed to perform the same role—protect you from fiscal harm. Look at your assets as if they are in layers, ordered according to their liquidity. First cash, mutual funds and money markets. Then stocks and bonds, the cash value of life insurance policies, real estate. As we noted earlier, good planning before you're in trouble means you have between six months and a year of savings available to cover the portion of your regular expenses that your check covered.

Some advisors argue that this money should be above and beyond your investments, a cash insurance policy against just this sort of disaster. Whether it is that, or an integral element of your investment plan that could be sacrificed if you lost your job, it is the outer layer of your defense. Use it first, then dip into your mutual fund. When that's gone, you can move on to stocks and bonds.

Before you liquidate any of your real estate, borrow against your cash value life insurance policy or consider refinancing your home. If interest rates are lower now than when you first took out your mortgage, you may be able to refinance at the more favorable rate and reduce your monthly costs. Or you could increase the size of the loan—that is, refinance for more than the balance due on your mortgage—so you have some cash from the deal. To avoid shelling out your valuable funds for the up-front costs of refinancing, you could roll the costs into the mortgage, or you might be able to find a "no point, no cost" loan, though the higher interest rates associated with such loans may negate any benefit of the deal. If you have a sufficient amount of equity in your home relative to its value, you might qualify for a home-equity line of credit. In either case, with refinancing or a home-equity line of credit, you'll have to meet the lender's income and debt requirements, which may be difficult even if your spouse is employed. If you have already established a line of home-equity credit, you could tap that, in an emergency, as long as you realize that the lender typically reserves the right to take a second look at your qualifications and that you are risking your home if you encounter any payback problems.

If you must sell land or buildings, bear in mind that those assets are less liquid than other assets. You will need more time, at least several months, before you have any money from them, so you must plan further ahead as time passes.

Don't dip into retirement funds unless your back is against the wall. In most instances, you're penalized for distributions, plus you owe income taxes on the money. That's

Every interview is a rehearsal for the one that does culminate in an offer.

If you don't get quick results, you needn't despair; finding a job will take more time than you want it to.

a stiff penalty for the cash you'll receive. In most instances, you'll owe the income tax due on it plus a 10% penalty. If you are between 55 and 59½ you can arrange for a regular payout of retirement funds and avoid the penalty.

Before you consider eliminating your assets, know that you can make arrangements with some of your creditors to reduce your monthly payments. Some loans can be extended, or the terms re-negotiated. Your mortgage holder may agree to smaller payments for a set period of time—no bank or savings & loan wants to end up owning your house. Many lenders have programs for people in just your circumstances that allow you to make partial payments for a time and make up the difference when you're back on your feet.

An important note: It is key for you to remember you must make the first move when you can't keep up with your bills. You lose goodwill as a bargaining chip when you wait for a bank or creditor to contact you regarding an overdue bill.

Maintain the Style

Your job gave you more than status. It gave you something to do, a sense of purpose. It was a daily ritual you will now probably sorely miss. Make your job search your job. In fact, you must if you want to move swiftly to a new position. Don't sleep in. Don't sit around the house in your bathrobe. Arise as you always did. Work a full morning making contacts, writing and calling, arranging interviews and going to them. Break for lunch, come home for dinner and do everything as if you were working—because you are. You haven't lost your job—you're looking for a new one.

Too many job seekers have destroyed their chances for jobs they could have had because they came into interviews with failure written all over their faces. It permeated their conversation, clouded their resume. An unemployed person carries a disadvantage into the interview that is a challenge to overcome even for those who are motivated. Nothing succeeds like success, and being without a job is not exactly the definition of that. But you can counter that. Your situation is not hopeless. Salespeople use a mind trick you can employ to counter the rejection you will invariably feel when you are turned down for a job. Regard those seeming setbacks as *rehearsals* for the interview that does culminate in an offer.

Second, if you maintain the momentum of work as you look for work, you will act as an *employed* person and in due—and hopefully swift—time you will be that in fact. (For more on how to keep your "gainfully employed" bearings, see Chapter 3.)

Outplacement firms stress this not only in their advice to job hunters but in the manner in which they treat their clients. If you go into an outplacement program, don't be surprised to find yourself carefully monitored, as if you were in school, with your homework—resumes, cover letters and interviews—graded sometimes every day. These professionals know from experience that keeping you pumped up plays two critical roles in finding you a new job.

First, if you've been in a position for a number of years you've probably lost all but the most basic job-hunting skills. An outplacement firm will refresh your skills. (Of course, we'll be sharpening them in later chapters on resumes, networking and interviewing.) You're not used to being both the product and the salesperson. For most people it is an acquired skill, one that must be practiced to be perfected.

Second, you may not realize just how many people you will have to see before the odds favor an offer. The ratio you'll hear at some outplacement firms runs like this: You'll need to contact with telephone calls and letters 50 firms for every interview you land. You'll require 10 interviews to get an offer. You should have three offers before you accept anything. That adds up to 1,500 inquiries and 30 interviews.

You probably won't send out 1,500 resumes—indeed you probably haven't done that in your life. And outplacement firms are big on developing and working many, *many* contacts. So your own experience will probably be closer to 50 or 60 resumes and contacts, and a dozen interviews. You'll probably get one or two offers and accept the best one without waiting to see what else comes in. But consider the initial numbers a parameter, a way to reassure you that if you don't get quick results, you needn't despair; finding a job will take more time than you want it to.

A 1993 Right Associates survey found that men and women middle managers took an average of 23 weeks to find a new position after they were notified they were losing their jobs. There's irony in these numbers. A study done in 1988 showed that female executives took an average of 16 weeks to find a new job; males 20 weeks. The Philadelphia outplacement firm said salary was the controlling factor and that women, who in the study earned 73% of what men earned in the same position, took less time to find another job because they were paid less. Today, with the pay gap closing at least some, the difference has disappeared.

You probably thought you could wrap this up with a couple of phone calls. Indeed you might, if your network is in top shape (see Chapter 9 for details). But lacking that, and most people do, your job search could take at least several months.

When You Want Out

Like those people who went straight to Chapter 2, you've got some time to maneuver, to consider what to do with your worklife. There may be writing on the wall, but it is not indelible. Still, you're aware that you are unhappy and you know that one day others will notice it too. You don't want to leave this condition untreated.

Your Winter of Discontent

If it were just a season, we might wait out a case of the job blues and hope for an early spring. But career pain is too intense for that. You have to do something about it, and quick. For some, that becomes a self-destructive spiral into missed work, confrontations with the boss and ultimately dismissal. Others drift into a smoky malaise their colleagues peg as burnout long before they realize what has happened. Like backwater in a bubbling stream, they sit placidly, unaware of just why it is they aren't moving.

Of course, before you clear up this logjam you have to find it. What's holding up your career? You? The job? A blocked promotion? Something else?

Any or all of these can sour you on work. Let's look at each to see what's bugging you.

Is It You?

In a sense it is always you. After all, someone else in your shoes might be grateful for the opportunity, might find the long hours invigorating, might (crazy as it sounds) actually get along with that goat in the front office. . .

But then again, maybe no one could be expected to like what you have, once they understood the circumstances you're working within. That's the first step in uncovering why you are unhappy with your job. You must understand the circumstances, separating them into factors within you and those that are endemic to your work or to life.

"I'm worried about you, Fred. I think you've been in the rat race too long!"

From The Wall Street Journal, Permission, Cartoon Features Syndicate

How have things changed?

Think back to the beginning of your career. Did things go well? Were you happy? Did your employers reward you with more responsibility, pay raises and promotions? Or has it always been a struggle for you to succeed?

If it has, maybe it's time to rethink what you do. Changing careers carries risk, but the rewards of greater satisfaction and a renewed chance for success are compelling enough reasons for the hundreds of thousands who do it each year.

From rock to investing: David Nelson's colleagues in the rock group The Turtles realized he was serious about a career change when he arrived for a concert in Kansas City in the early 1990s without waist-length hair. After 13 years with the group known for such hits as "Happy Together" and "She'd Rather Be With Me," Nelson had had enough. He wanted to make money, not music.

Nelson made the switch to financial consultant with Merrill Lynch, a large New York brokerage. After training, his pay could easily top $150,000 annually, more than he was making as a musician.

Nelson knew his days in rock 'n' roll were numbered when, in the mid '80s, he toted up everything that was making him dissatisfied. His hearing had been damaged from years of playing in front of booming speakers. He was disillusioned with pop music, which seemed less of an art form than when he started his musical career in Berkeley in the late '60s. He had seen too many fellow musicians wind up broke in a business that's supposed to spawn millionaires. "I saw my colleagues ripped off all the time," he says. "I swore that would never happen to me."

Nelson found he enjoyed taking an active role in the Turtles' investments and by 1987 was ready for a move. But his timing stunk. The stock market crashed and brokers flooded the unemployment lines. He stayed with the band while getting his broker's license. When the economy improved in 1991, he headed for the barbershop and then for an interview with the brokerage.

He faced rejection if he couldn't make a solid argument for how a rocker could succeed as a broker. "I knew I had the credentials and the understanding," he says. "I told them nothing was more competitive than the music business and that I had made it there for a very long time." As he talked his way into the new field, Nelson also reminded prospective employers that he had managed the money for the production companies he ran.

Nelson thinks his age was an asset: "When you are 44 and you decide to make a career change, they think you must be pretty committed to doing it."

Nelson's boss at Merrill Lynch, Linda Marcelli, agrees. "He had good business sense and understood how to manage money. He had good long-term relationships in the music business and people trusted him."

What are you pretending you don't know?

In Chapter 4 you'll find information on vocational testing and pursuing alternative careers, while Chapter 5 helps you think about starting your own business. These are all avenues you should consider if you see a common thread of discord and failure in your career.

At the same time, your pattern of failure may come from factors that will not change with a new job. You're kidding yourself by escaping into the future, only to find yourself again unsatisfied and again searching for the per-

You're kidding yourself by escaping into the future, only to find yourself again unsatisfied and again searching for the perfect job.

You may be a victim of one or more of what are probably the three most common sources of internal unrest: stress, burn-out or depression.

fect job. Now may be the time to take stock of how you do business. You may discover deeper-seated problems that should be dealt with. Delving into that area is beyond the scope of this book but your physician or a mental health professional may be able to help you better understand your actions and feelings.

Worn out and just plain pooped

There's a third situation that may describe you. You once liked your job but now find it unrewarding. You may be a victim of one or more of what are probably the three most common sources of internal unrest: stress, burnout or depression. You picked the right field, you just worked it one season too long. You're fallow, in need of a rest, your faculties depleted. You may feel like a basket case but you can be treated.

To help you peg your problem, here's a brief outline of each of these maladies. Often you can treat stress yourself; burnout sometimes, but depression, if it's diagnosed as clinical, probably not. Your physician or a mental health specialist may be able to help you devise a response or treatment for whichever ails you. Many employers offer stress clinics that help you cope.

Stress

Everyone feels stress. A little can be a powerful incentive. It's tension, and in mild doses and under the right circumstances, it is your competitive edge, sharpening your senses, honing your reaction time. The late Canadian researcher Dr. Hans Selye was the first to "discover" and label stress in humans in the 1930s. Not long after, he concluded humans ought to have a little of it in their lives to keep them interested. But too much stress is overload.

You're wound up and it is hard to calm down. There's too much work to do (or too many family or personal obligations). You're missing deadlines, you're angry and irritable and now you're finding it hard to make decisions. As it worsens, you'll start missing work, you will be prone to accidents and you may begin abusing drugs and alcohol. Much of the illness you'll encounter—colds, physical aches and pains—will be attributed to your stress. Your blood pressure may rise, you'll have tension in your jaw and neck muscles. You'll feel light-headed sometimes, have chills and unexpected perspiration and a racing pulse. Keep at it long enough and you'll discover that stress is the preamble to burnout.

Stress can kill you (the thought of which is probably stress-inducing in itself). A study of 50-year-old men in Sweden showed just how lethal stress in certain settings can be. The study covered seven years ending in 1993 and included interviews with the subjects at the beginning of the study. In the interviews the men were asked if they had strong family ties or social support systems. They were also asked if any of a series of life events had recently happened to them. Seven years later, the researchers combed official records to find which of their subjects had died. They matched the dead with their responses in the earlier interviews. The researchers discovered that men who had reported three or more recent upsetting life events—such as concerns for a family member, being forced to move, serious financial problems, being the target of a legal action and insecurity at work—were the most likely to die among the men in the study. It's easy to paint a picture of a man beset with problems at work, who is thus worried about money, having concerns as a result about a family member, and being forced to move to reduce expenses or to relocate. And ultimately paying with his life for the resulting stress. How? It wasn't a direct psychological link, interestingly, but researchers surmised that a lowered resistance to disease was brought on by the stress. Emotionally reassuring relationships can act to buffer the effects of stress. While the study looked only at men, earlier studies in the U.S. have included both men and women and they, too, show a link between social ties and mortality, that is, strong social ties can help resist the ravages of physically wearing conditions such as stress.

Curious about your own level of stress? No doubt, especially if you're among those people who have fewer friends and loose family ties. Take a few minutes now to go to page 48. Take the stress test there and see how you're doing.

Stress can kill you (the thought of which is probably stress-inducing in itself).

Continued on page 51

Test Your Stress

Change, any change, means stress. But some changes affect us more than others. Dr. Richard Rahe of the Nevada Stress Center devised this scale. He found that if you score 301 or more points worth of change experienced during the past six months, you run a high risk of illness.

Life Event	Value	Your Score
Health		
An injury or illness which kept you in bed a week or more, or in the hospital	42	_____
Major dental work	40	_____
Major change in sleeping habits	31	_____
Major change in usual type and/or amount of recreation	30	_____
Major change in eating habits	29	_____
An injury or illness that was less serious than described in first item, above	25	_____
Work		
Fired from work	64	_____
Laid off from work	57	_____
A demotion at work	57	_____
Retirement	49	_____
Troubles with your boss	39	_____
Major business adjustment	38	_____
Change to a new type of work	38	_____
A transfer at work	38	_____
Troubles with your co-workers	35	_____
Change in work hours and conditions	33	_____
More responsibilities at work	31	_____
A promotion at work	31	_____
Work troubles other than those described here	31	_____
Troubles with persons under your supervision	30	_____
Fewer responsibilities at work	29	_____
Correspondence course	29	_____

Home and Family

Death of spouse	105	_____
Death of a child	105	_____
Death of parent	66	_____
Death of sibling	64	_____
Divorce	62	_____
Pregnancy	60	_____
Relative moves in with you	57	_____
You separate from your spouse due to marital problems	56	_____
Miscarriage or abortion	53	_____
Major change in health or behavior of family member	52	_____
Marriage	50	_____
You separate from your spouse due to work	49	_____
New family member by birth	49	_____
New family member by adoption	45	_____
Marital reconciliation	42	_____
Major change in living conditions	39	_____
Change in residence to a different town, city or state	38	_____
Your parents divorce	38	_____
Spouse beginning or ending work outside the home	37	_____
Change in arguments with spouse	34	_____
Your parents remarry	33	_____
Birth of grandchild	31	_____
Child leaving home for marriage	30	_____
Child leaving home for reasons other than those described here	29	_____
In-law problems	29	_____
Change in residence within same town or city	28	_____
Child leaving home for college	28	_____
Change in family get-togethers	26	_____

Continued on page 50

Test Your Stress (cont'd.)

Personal and Social

Being held in jail	57	_____
Sexual difficulties	49	_____
Death of a close friend	46	_____
Major decision regarding the immediate future	45	_____
An accident	44	_____
Engagement to marry	39	_____
"Falling out" of a close personal relationship	35	_____
Major personal achievement	33	_____
Beginning or ending school or college	32	_____
Minor violation of the law	32	_____
New, close, personal relationship	32	_____
Change in personal habits	31	_____
Girlfriend or boyfriend problems	30	_____
Change in religious beliefs	29	_____
Vacation	29	_____
Change of school or college	28	_____
Change in social activities	28	_____
Change in political beliefs	25	_____

Financial

Major change in finances—decreased income	60	_____
Foreclosure on a mortgage or loan	57	_____
Major change in finances due to investment and/or credit difficulties	43	_____
Loss or damage of personal property	40	_____
Major purchase	39	_____
Major change in finances—increased income	27	_____
Moderate purchase	26	_____

Your Total

_____

Note: If you score 301 or more you have a high risk of illness; 201-300, an elevated risk; 126-200, a moderate risk; and 0-125, a low risk.

Where Stress Is

It seems like it's everywhere some days. But in your career you'll most often find it in situations where:

- **You feel you don't have the staff, resources or power you need to do your job.**

- **You don't believe you are receiving enough recognition,** monetary or otherwise, for the work you do. The American Management Association found in a study that lack of feedback about one's performance was a major cause of stress.

- **You feel your path is blocked** by the bureaucracy in your company, by political pressures or a lack of information.

The bottom line is that you feel blocked, thwarted in your attempts to do what you believe can otherwise be a highly fulfilling activity—your work.

Stress is serious enough for some people to seek compensation from their employers, although the trend has abated, in great part because laws defining stress have been narrowed. Still, stress claims are among the lengthiest of worker compensation claims—where there's an award, the average claim is for 39 weeks. (The average claim for an occupational disease lasted 36 weeks; traumatic injuries 24 weeks.) Clearly, when stress hits a worker, that person is down for a long count. Women are as likely as men to file mental stress claims. By comparison, only 33% of injury claims are made by women according to the National Council on Compensation Insurance. Fewer claims since the law changed doesn't mean stress is less prevalent in the workplace. The National Institute of Occupational Safety and Health says stress is now one of the ten leading work-related problems.

What You Can Do About Stress

Take a walk.

Chief among them, aside from reducing the source of stress, is physical exercise. The American Heart Association

The bottom line is that you feel blocked, thwarted in your attempts to do what you believe can otherwise be a highly fulfilling activity—your work.

Make a shorter list, finish an item at a time. Or skip the list. Just work steadily.

says just walking, three to four times a week for thirty to sixty minutes each time can make a difference in how you cope with stress and on the level of health you enjoy. If you're over 40, however, be sure to precede any exercise program with a physician's check-up.

Cut your list.

A second important way to deal with stress is to look at how much you try to cram into a day. Maybe that list of 14 items isn't realistic. Perhaps you're trying to get something done on each item and succeeding in finishing none. That's a formula for stress. Make a shorter list, finish an item at a time. Or skip the list and just work steadily, which may bring us to another way to deal with stress.

Make the most of your time.

You can learn to manage your time more efficiently. Consider how much time you spend in lines, how often you're fidgeting while you wait for something, a call, perhaps, or materials from the copy machine. Learn to fill in those blanks with other activities or design your schedule so you miss the lines.

Think—again.

Raising your self-esteem can reduce stress, as can deciding to take a more positive approach to your work. Plenty of people have discovered among the rewards of middle age is a better understanding that life is pretty much what you make of it. You don't have to be facing 40 to change your thinking, however.

Are you a complainer more from habit than condition? This is not a tome of pop psychology, but too often much of our complaining is from habit, not from a genuine dissatisfaction. You may also be picking up the attitudes of colleagues who are complainers. Steer clear of them.

Do you act on impulse rather than waiting out an emotion or a reaction? Wait a few minutes before replying to, say, an e-mail message that seems too flip for your taste. Count to ten before you speak if you feel your anger rising. Wait to respond to a memo that has your dander up. Silence will damn you far fewer times than your words.

Are you asking more from your job and your colleagues than they can reasonably be asked? Because we spend so much time with our colleagues, sometimes more than with family or certainly more than with friends, it is easy to mistake the workplace for family. There is power in feeling professional comradeship, but the office is not your home, nor are your colleagues your family. They don't have to like you in order to work effectively with you.

Get a life.

Are you turning yourself into a single entity: an employee? Certainly your career is a critical part of your life, but it shouldn't be the only factor in your sense of well-being. Remember those lonely Swedes in the stress study. Family, religion, friends, hobbies, a commitment to volunteer work, travel—all of these can add richness to your life and place your work in its proper context. A balanced life also improves your sense of value as you draw positive reinforcement from a number of sources, not simply your boss. And, not incidentally, a network of support may produce job leads come the time when you need them.

Other Ways to Reduce Stress

• •

- **A balanced diet,** three meals a day, weight control, no snacking between meals.

- **Regular exercise,** at least 30 minutes a day at least five times a week, and you can break up the exercises into shorter sessions. Even brisk walking is effective for reducing stress.

- **Relaxation exercises,** including massage and yoga.

- **Cut caffeine** from your menu.

- **Don't smoke.**

- **Take a stress-reduction seminar.** Many companies regularly offer them to help employees cope with stress.

- **Reach out.** Your family (at least the part that isn't causing stress), a member of the clergy, your doctor, friends, can all help you cope with stress, too.

Burnout

Let's assume there was a time when you enjoyed your work. You enjoyed the job you have now. You took pleasure in the challenge, saw rewards and thought of new chal-

You never came back from an exhausting project. Your zest evaporated. Your ideas just stopped. You're all too aware of what time it is. You're burned out.

lenges. You were on fire for the task, or at least good and warm toward what you were doing. You were a team player, in fact if not in spirit, your goals in harmony with your company's. Work and play and the rest of your life were a seamless time from dawn to the moment you put your head to your pillow at night.

Then something happened. You never came back from an exhausting project. Your zest for the business at hand evaporated. The flow of ideas from your brain just seemed to stop. At any given moment now you have an accurate notion of the time, and of how much time remains before lunch, before you can quit, before you must return to work.

If you read the preceding two paragraphs and found yourself in them, then it is probably time to acknowledge your own case of burnout. You've worked too hard for too long and there isn't much of you left to rally around anything. You are killing time on the job and if you're not careful, it's going to hurt you. Burnout is common in an age of workaholics, cut-throat competition and layoffs.

Two California psychologists, Ayala Pines and Elliot Aronson, claim credit for coining the phrase in a 1981 book, *Burnout: From Tedium to Personal Growth* and expanded on it in *Career Burnout: Causes and Cures* (Free Press) in 1988. (Both titles are now out of print; check your local library.)

They said burnout was a state of physical, emotional and mental exhaustion caused by long-term involvement in situations that are emotionally demanding. They linked high expectations and chronic stress.

Most susceptible are people who identify too much with their work. Because they see competition as a threat, they respond to crisis with anxiety, aggression and hostility. And of course they see competition as a threat because they too strongly identify with their work. On and on the cycle goes until the victim is burned out.

Women face special dilemmas created by their upbringing and society's expectation that they will be responsible for home as well as a career if they choose to work and have a family. There's an often fatal one-two punch in that women tend to seek more self-fulfillment from their jobs but see careers as "the future" and their job as "the present." Men, on the other hand, see each job as part of a series that makes up their career. If one job falters, like a wobbly stone in a pathway across a creek, men simply jump to the next, in the hope it will be steadier. Women, with a short-range view and more on the line emotionally, suffer job failures more acutely. It's as if, not seeing the next stone to jump to, they sink where they stand. As a result, more women than men burn out on the job.

You can count depression, feelings of alienation, malaise, increased illness and aimlessness among its manifestations. "Burnouts" are more accident prone, suffer through more colds, headaches and flu. Their backs and shoulders ache from tension, they're tired all day but sleep poorly at night. They are more critical of their work than others are of their own. They have seen their eating habits change, they are lonely and discouraged and some think about suicide. It's a real top-to-bottom formula for trouble. Don't confuse it with stress. The difference is how you feel, or don't feel, at the end of a day. It's stress if you still have some sense of significance, however frustrated you may feel. You still argue for improvement and hope your goals can be somehow achieved. If those feelings are gone, you are probably burned out.

It's possible to fake burnout. Lazy people were doing it long before it had a name. But it's hard to cover it up if you suffer from it. By its very nature it can leave you paralyzed. As with depression, you can't simply will it away in a day or two. You have to break the cycle that is creating it. That may mean changing jobs, so you'll want to pay close attention to the symptoms outlined here to see if you are burned out or in danger of burning out.

To Learn More

• •

You can find plenty of texts that deal with stress. (If a book is out of print, chances are you can still find it at your public library or a used book store.)

- *Beyond Machiavelli: Tools for Coping with Conflict,* by Roger Fisher (Penguin).

- *Games Mother Never Taught You: Corporate Gamesmanship for Women,* by Betty Lehan Harragan (Warner), and

- *Healthy People in Unhealthy Places: Stress and Fitness at Work,* by Kenneth R. Pelletier (Delta; out of print).

Burnout is hard to cover up. It can leave you paralyzed, and you can't just quickly will it away. You have to break the cycle that's creating it.

What You Can Do

First, you don't have to blame yourself. Most burnout is situational. That is, you change the situation, you end the burnout. No sessions on the psychiatrist's couch, no stays in the sanitarium. But this doesn't mean *you* don't have to change, too. Shifting to a new job may break the chain of 60-hour weeks and lift you out of burnout. But changing jobs won't keep you immune from burnout if you go back to 60-hour weeks in a few months.

For Deborah Coleman, who was a high-powered chief financial officer at Apple Computer, getting off the merry-go-round was the solution. Announcing she wanted a more balanced life than the one she had, she stepped down for a two-month leave of absence (that eventually stretched to five months). In that time she traveled, exercised and re-modeled her kitchen.

She made it plain her leave was not an admission of failure, but a recognition that she needed a break from work, one that left her once more revved up about her career. Former Apple Chairman John Scully endorsed the move by taking his own six-week sabbatical and by extending an invitation for her to return to a less demanding position, which she did. (Coleman later left the company, as did Scully.) Ms. Coleman's move was drastic, to be sure, but it highlighted the destructiveness of a high-pressure job. Your own circumstances may not allow you to do what she did, but you can deal with burnout in other effective ways.

Change your response.

As we noted, this is one of the most effective strategies. Stop being surprised by what is a predictable situation. At 10:58 P.M. in a television newsroom there will be tension as everyone readies for the 11 P.M. broadcast. It's not realistic to be surprised by that.

You can change the situation.

Don't be in a television newsroom at 10:58 P.M. Negotiate for the day shift, so you're working to complete an assignment, not to beat the clock.

Make your own time as precious as your work time.

Don't work weekends except in emergencies. Quit work each day at the same time and don't let the work week creep upward over time. Studies have shown you're at your best for no more than an eight hour day. Work longer and you forfeit efficiency.

Make active—not passive—responses.

Bargaining for a better situation is an active response. Getting drunk every night is not. Remember that you've been a valued employee and your boss probably would like nothing better than to see you back to your old highly effective self, too. You may get a temporary rearrangement of responsibilities, or even a different position in the company, that will give you the time to renew yourself.

Depression

The news about the blues is that it's around more than you may realize. Some 9.4 million Americans will suffer clinical depression during any six-month period, according to the American Psychiatric Association. One in eight of us will be clinically depressed at some time in our lives. This means we will show the signs of depression—listlessness, weight loss, irritability and a host of other, and sometimes opposite, symptoms—for a month or more. Despite our most willful efforts, these feelings will not go away. At its worst, you will feel hopeless and you may even consider suicide.

Women are more likely than men to be depressed (although older widowed or divorced men are the most likely to attempt and succeed at suicide), single people more than married, unemployed more than employed. But depression's source may go deeper into our psyches. For some of us, it may be unavoidable, its origins embedded in our genes. Researchers have found that heredity does play a part. If you have a parent or sibling who suffers depression, there is a greater likelihood that you will as well. Depressed people also tend to think about depression too much, con-

One in eight of us will be clinically depressed at sometime in our lives.

Another trigger of depression—exit events over which you have no control but that exclude you from society... like getting fired or laid off.

tributing to the condition. Indeed, part of the cure in psychiatry is an attempt to refocus a patient's attention on other things.

Life events may also all but guarantee an onset of depression. Studies have labeled four predictors as vulnerability factors:

- Lack of a confiding relationship with someone.

- Having three or more children under the age of 14.

- The childhood loss of a parent through death or separation.

- And, of interest to you, unemployment.

Another trigger—*exit events* over which you have no control but which exclude you from society...like getting fired or laid off.

Depression comes in several forms—some is persistent, some a roller coaster of highs and lows. Your concern is how to measure its severity and what to do about it. Mild depression will often go away of its own accord. Depression requires more attention when you lose interest in the usual activities. You take no pleasure in life, you can't sleep, you feel guilt and worthlessness. If these symptoms last more than two weeks, you may be experiencing clinical depression. You should see your family doctor or a clinic that deals with psychological disorders.

Depending on the severity of the depressed state, treatment may include drugs that level your moods, psychotherapy or, in extreme situations, a combination of the two and electro-convulsive treatment.

For most people, improvement comes within a month, and most depressions end within a year. More than half of those who have suffered clinical depression will have subsequent episodes.

Despite the ease with which many forms of depression can be treated, it is often undiagnosed by doctors. A study done by Dr. Kenneth Wells, a psychiatrist at the University of California at Los Angeles, found severe depression went undiagnosed about half of the time. Patients seeing private physicians on a fee-for-service basis fared better than those patients using prepaid services such as health maintenance organizations, the study found. This suggests that perhaps you should raise the possibility of depression with your doctor even when you don't believe it could be a part of your problem.

Focusing on these three common workplace problems may help you uncover your unhappiness. Or you may discover by their absence that your problems lie outside of you.

The average number of times that we change jobs is being skewed upward by basic changes in the workplace.

When the Problem Isn't You

We change jobs on average eight times in our working lives, although for most of us that figure includes a jumble of low-rung positions at the beginning of our careers that we are happy to leave followed by a relatively lengthy and stable tenure with one or two firms where presumably we grow professionally and prosper. That's the average, but the numbers are being skewed upward by basic changes in the workplace that we touched upon in the beginning pages of this book. Those changes bear careful consideration here as you search for answers to your discontent.

- **International competition is blurring the lines between what is *domestic* and what is *foreign*.** American companies now see much of their growth overseas. That means more growth there than here, flatter careers for Americans who stay at home, and value to those with foreign experience and language skills.

- **Mergers and acquisitions are thrusting hundreds of thousands of people into new high stress situations.** Just ask bank employees, electronics technicians and telecommunications professionals who are facing new employers, or layoffs, where stress fits into their lives. Few companies that merge are as big collectively as they were before the marriage.

- **Huge cuts in defense spending have put hundreds of thousands of skilled and semi-skilled workers and management level employees on the street.** Add to that the thousands of career military personnel who are being mustered out of the Army, Navy, Air Force and Marines.

Look at the company where you work. How is it doing? Business is strong? Holding its own? Losing ground?

Then there is the tremendous impact base closing and defense industry shrinkage has on communities, and the thousands of people who indirectly are supported by defense spending.

- **This is all occurring in a sluggish worldwide economy while big U.S. corporations continue a seemingly endless stream of layoffs.**

This means that besides analyzing yourself, you must also begin to appreciate how much the outside world may be putting a crimp on your career. There is little need to deal with conditions where you work if your corporation is headed for bankruptcy or breakup because of basic changes in your industry or world economics.

Changes in Your Industry

Is your industry threatened by trends or is it on a winning track? The latter half of the decade is a time of mergers in key industries like banking and breakups for giants such as ITT and AT&T. Many U.S. corporations are banking on overseas markets to fuel growth in the rest of this decade. Europe, the Pacific Rim, Japan—these are the markets that are seen as having the greatest potential for growth. Is your industry building business in those markets or responding effectively to competition from those countries?

Where in its typical business cycle is your industry? American auto makers are regaining the market share they lost in the last decade, though they are now coming off boom times and facing a slowdown in sales. American banks are in a merger frenzy that's putting thousands of middle managers out of work. Telecommunications giants like BellSouth are ruthlessly downsizing to be more profitable. High-tech firms like Sun Microsystems are growing on the explosive expansion of the Internet. Workers in these businesses know how these conditions are affecting their jobs. An aerospace engineer understands that her industry is in tough times, for example, and she must be prepared for no promotion, maybe no raise, maybe even a layoff. A Boeing engineer denying these factors, such a common practice when times are tough, can be frustrated into unhappiness in the same situation.

Your Company

Now look at the company where you work. How is it doing? Business is strong? Holding its own? Losing ground? Smart employees today follow their company's performance in the business trade press. They read the quarterly and annual reports. They own company stock and read analysts' reports from their brokers. They are tapped into the company grapevine and know about new products and how existing products are doing. Kimberly-Clark employees know, for example, that while business is booming for the paper industry, a merger with Scott Paper will mean thousands of their jobs are not secure, and their working climate reflects that.

The Boss

And at the very closest level, who's the boss? The person who hired you and promoted you or someone new? Someone who might want to build his or her own team. How has your relationship progressed? Are you still considered part of the team?

Your discontent may come from other kinds of change. It may be that you were misled on what the job would be. It's not uncommon for an employer with a hot prospect to oversell a job to lure a person on board. Maybe you've been baited into a slot for which no one has any real hope you'll succeed or with which you will be satisfied. Serve your time, but don't take the outcome personally.

Time may have played a part. When you started, the combination of your skills and the job were a match that served the company well. Your company's needs may have changed since then. You're in marketing, for example, in a company that now needs more expertise on logistics—on moving raw materials, or shipping finished product.

A merger or the latest round of cutbacks may have played havoc with your job title. You may have ended up

Corporate cutbacks can dim long-range career plans for survivors.

Don't discount the culture. You may just be out of sync with the place where you work.

with a lesser job, less autonomy, fewer responsibilities and a shrunken title.

Corporate cutbacks can dim long-range career plans for the survivors, derail your career track and leave you in danger of becoming redundant, the one-too-many manager whose name will turn up on the next layoff list.

Don't discount the culture. You may just be out of sync with the place where you work. You're loud, now everyone else is the strong, silent type. You're from South Carolina; after the new boss came in three years ago your co-workers all seem to be from the Bronx. Or maybe it's a matter of scale. You function best with a solid organization behind you but now you work with a bunch of cowboys who think an answering machine is as much backup as anyone could need.

Discrimination May Be Hurting You

You may be facing any of several kinds of discrimination. Your age, sex, religion, race—all can be used against you illegally, and not always so blatantly that you realize what's happening. Proving discrimination can be difficult. If you believe you have been a victim of discrimination, you can discuss the matter with a representative of the Equal Employment Opportunity Commission in the city where you live, although that process will be slow. Your own organization may have a person or department with responsibility for adhering to federal and state equal opportunity laws. You can talk with an attorney who specializes in discrimination cases. Your local bar association can give you names.

For Women, Other Factors

Many women face all of the challenges and setbacks that come when they choose work in male-dominated fields such as manufacturing or real estate development. Outplacement experts Madeleine and Robert Swain say women have four choices in these situations:

- They can leave in search of a more accepting field,

- They can become one of the boys,

- They can try to adapt to the existing culture, or

- They can try to become a trailblazer, forcing the organization to change.

None is accomplished without personal sacrifice and commitment.

Some sense of the frustration for women can be seen from a survey of 26,500 men and women at seven corporations completed by Opinion Research Corp. in Princeton, N.J. The study showed that it was not conflicts between work and family that prompted women to quit work or change jobs. Instead, they said it was because they were blocked from promotion or treated poorly by their bosses. This by now familiar glass ceiling (so named because women could see beyond their own stymied ambitions to positions in the hierarchy occupied by men no more qualified than they were) was cited by the study's authors as the reason women were more likely to leave a job than men.

Schwadron, Cartoonists & Writers Syndicate

Your Plan

By now, you should have a fair understanding of your contribution to the problem and how your job and occupation contribute to your feelings. While much of the mist shrouding the issues may have cleared, the bottom-line question remains: What should you do about it?

Obviously, you can stay or you can leave. If you stay, how can you change things so you like it where you are? If you leave, where will you go? Much of the rest of this book deals with the latter course of action, so let's focus for a time on staying.

Find your own mentor informally— within or outside of the company.

Making a Stand Where You Are

Staying isn't necessarily a bad idea, even if it isn't in vogue. A study conducted in the late 1980s by Korn/Ferry International and UCLA's John E. Anderson Graduate School of Management found the surest way to the top was to climb through the ranks. Fully 80 percent of all corporate promotions came from within the company. Staying with a company means continuing in its pension plan, stock-option, profit-sharing and other programs that are often designed to discourage job switching. Start at a new company and you may be starting over for eligibility in many of these plans—even if you're picking up a hefty salary increase.The key is to know if your company rewards those who stay. Make a census of those who were promoted in the last couple of years where you work. Find out how long they've been with the company. A career that spans more than a decade in one place suggests your company rewards longevity. A host of newcomers getting ahead is a sure sign it doesn't.

Of course if you stay put, you probably will have to make some changes. You're professing your unhappiness, after all. If you diagnosed a case of burnout, a shift in responsibilities may be required. If stress is a factor, an exercise program and better management of your time will be the key to success. Depression often ends with the passage of time but you should consider therapy if the condition is chronic or severe.

More Ways to Stay Put

Mentoring, inside or outside

You can repair your career other ways, too. Your company may have programs in place to accomplish just that. For example, Johnson & Johnson and AT&T Bell Laboratories have had formal mentor programs aimed at matching senior managers with junior managers. Senior managers play corporate coaches—guiding, counseling and protecting their protégés as they do their work. Mentors have played invaluable roles in the ascension of countless executives, clearing paths up through the ranks for a chosen few. That kind of direct but relatively non-threatening communication could restore your connection with the company.

If there is no mentoring program where you work, that doesn't stop you from finding your own mentor informally. You may want to target your mentor within or outside of the company. As you seek out those in senior ranks for the role, be certain your candidates are interested in your career, are willing to give advice (even beyond your tenure with the company), know your organization well enough to

Marcia Auberger: From Temp to Perm

For more than five years Marcia Auberger practiced family law in Galveston, Texas. But a half decade of divorce and child custody cases was enough and in early 1995, she headed for Washington, D.C., intent on finding a new law practice. Auberger targeted the government and the many professional and non-profit associations in the area but found nothing. Soon, she was temping through three employment firms that specialize in placing attorneys. She used the experience to check out various firms and types of practice.

Legal "temps" has become big business as law firms, looking to cut costs, hire on professionals for the duration of a particular case. The temporary—or "contract"— attorneys review documents, interview witnesses and help prepare cases for trial. Auberger is a dedicated attorney who loves the law, but even she said the hours were grueling and the work sometimes stultifying. But when she answered the telephones at one temp agency for a day when she was between assignments, she saw the literally hundreds of resumes that the agency received *each day*. "That made me feel grateful for what I had," she says.

After six months she got lucky, snagging a long-term assignment with the Washington, D.C. office of a Baltimore, Md. law firm. As it

happened, she was flown back to Texas to work on a false advertising/deceptive trade case and given a great deal of responsibility. "They didn't treat me like a temp," she says. "They genuinely valued my opinion."

When the case closed, the firm's managing partner took her aside to discuss a permanent position with the firm. Today she works in the firm's intellectual property area, chiefly on trademark and patent cases.

Landing a new and interesting position is the unabashed goal today for most temporary workers. Like Auberger, they were unhappy with their old job but unsure of what to do next. They took temp jobs both to pay the rent and to check out new careers. And because employers now embrace temping as a way to try out prospective employees, the plan is even endorsed by temping agencies which can tout the quality of their people by the rate of hires.

"Temping allowed me to prove myself," says Auberger. "This is an Ivy League firm, and temping helped me get my foot into an otherwise closed door. I knew if people could see how hard I work and what I can do, then they'd consider hiring me. I just needed that opportunity."

guide you through the politics of promotion, have access to key people and give you credit for your accomplishments.

"It happens to the best of us. Young turk one day, old turkey the next."

From The Wall Street Journal, Permission, Cartoon Features Syndicate

Your company may have re-training programs open to employees who want different jobs or who work in divisions slated for cutback or elimination. AT&T, for example, offers employees cut from one division the chance to train and work as temporary employees in other divisions. You may also suggest that your company hire a consulting firm such as Equinox Group. Created by career guru Tom Jackson, Equinox offers programs that teach employees how to take charge of their career planning and how to find satisfaction in their work.

Books that can help

Do-it-yourself advice comes from psychologist Carole Kanchier in *Care to Change Your Job and Your Life* (JIST Works). Not surprisingly, perhaps, she puts a strong psychological spin on getting your head straight first, then re-shaping your career.

A second book worth reading is *The Career Decisions Planner* by Joan Lloyd (John Wiley & Sons). Lloyd, a Milwaukee-based career consultant, peppers her book with quizzes designed to help you pinpoint the source of your unhappiness. Among her pieces of advice: Got a boss you can't stand? Give him or her a year before you throw in the towel. "If you like your work and enjoy the team of people with whom you work, I'd suggest you stay on the job for a while," she writes. "Let your new boss settle in…"

Authors William Lundin and Kathleen Lundin make an understandable path for dealing with tough colleagues in *Working with Difficult People* (Amacom). The book, mercifully concise, offers workbook-like exercises that help you identify the problem and deal with it.

If you like taking tests, try *Rate Your Executive Potential*, by Roger Fritz (John Wiley & Sons; out of print; check your local library). Fritz includes self-evaluation quizzes and action plans. If you want ultimate productivity, Fritz argues, manage your time meticulously, mapping out your day's work before you get to the office and know what you want to accomplish each week. Delegate as much work as possible, he says, and you will have the time you need to meet your goals.

Talking to the Top (Prentice Hall) author Ray Anthony, a professional trainer of presentation skills, offers methods for making effective presentations, a part of the work life long ignored. With communications skills so critical to career development, his advice is good for anyone—whether you have to make a presentation or not.

Want to catch a glimpse of the great workplace trends of the next century? Author Joseph Boyett continues his treatise on the future in *Beyond Workplace 2000* (Dutton), the follow-up to *Workplace 2000*. No revelations—teams replacing hierarchies, more flexibility in responding to the needs of the customer—but Boyett, himself a consultant on change to many Fortune 500 companies, offers a concise map for threading your way through the challenges of 2000 and beyond.

A friendly conference

Don't rule out talking with your boss or whoever is the source of your trouble at work. Conversation has been known to unravel what could be essentially meaningless differences and misunderstandings. Plan on meeting in a neutral place, a restaurant neither of you regularly frequents or a conference room in a part of the building where you do not go. No one will have the advantage or intimidation of surroundings.

You should pilot your course of action and stick to an agenda. Decide beforehand to clear as much of the emotion as you can from the setting. Be ready and truly willing to give up something or to concede something. Successful negotia-

The world, and certainly the world in which you work, is a small place—and it's getting smaller. No bridge-burning exits, please.

If you can't finish a project, leave it organized so your co-workers can pick up the reins.

tion will result only when both parties feel they have achieved something. Assume from the start both of you want resolution and state that first thing. Assume you have misunderstood one another in the past, make it plain you believe there is common ground the two of you can reach. But be prepared to cut the proceedings short if you believe the intent of the meeting has changed.

If your initial meeting is successful, plan to keep talking to one another in a similar spirit. You probably need not have any more "summits" but don't let the past repeat itself.

When Leaving Seems Best

Of course, you don't have to talk to anyone. You can leave knowing that's an acceptable course for a lot of people. Says Daniel Nagy, who is placement director at the Fuqua School of Business at Duke University, "Most people [who are unsatisfied] have stayed too long. Most should leave."

You may find that a bit abrupt but a little shaking up every five or six years keeps you fresh with energy and ideas. More importantly, it will energize your skills. In the '90s, offering current, marketable skills is key to survival in a downsizing, or when you're competing for promotions. Besides, staying at a company when you aren't growing is a sign you're in the wrong company, one that is vulnerable to competition.

You're Leaving

You tried mentors, you reduced the stress in your life and you tried to shift to a different department. Nothing worked. You want out. But don't leave this chapter until you've learned how to properly part company. However tempting it may be to make your closing speech from the top of your desk—and at the top of your lungs—don't. It pays to follow a certain protocol when you leave a job. Whether you want to admit it or not, you haven't met these folks for the last time. The world, and certainly the world in which you work, is a small place—and it's getting smaller. Don't wipe out half the power of your network of friends and associates with a bridge-burning exit from where you are.

Check your finances.

Unlike somebody who was forced from the job, you have some say over the timing of your departure. If all goes well, that will come after you've got the next job nailed down. But things sometimes don't work out so smoothly. You could find yourself out of your old job and without a new one. Even if you don't think this could happen, plan for it. Refer to the worksheets on pages 36 and 37 in Chapter 2 to measure your assets and cash flow. You should have at least six months of your salary in cash reserves or in investments you can tap without penalty—whether you're leaving a job or not.

Polish your record.

On any given day most of us are involved in more than a single project. We're cleaning up the loose ends from one, planning another, in the thick of a third. On and on we labor, knitting these strands of work into a record of accomplishments. But slice off your tenure with an abrupt exit and a lot of things aren't going to be finished, or even presentable. You're about to give notice of your departure. It's the time to shift from taking on work to finishing what you have underway. If you can't finish a project, leave it organized so your co-workers can pick up the reins. Mend your fences before you give notice, too. If you're not speaking to the principal accountant in finance, clear the air before the word is out that you're out.

Be discreet.

You'll also need to plan for interviews and time on the phone setting up appointments. You may need to dedicate your breaks and lunch hours to this task, plotting meetings for late in the day when you can slip away on comp time or by taking brief amounts of personal leave. If your job permits more freedom away from your desk, you can of course

Hope for a good-bye lunch, but prepare for the possibility that you will be asked to leave now.

be more flexible. But play by the rules where you work. You don't want to raise questions about your actions before you are ready to move.

Same holds true for long distance phone charges and using the company copying machine. In fact, stay away from any services like that available in your office. Don't use the fax or the printer. Forget to pick up something and you have revealed your plans. That could cost you where you are, leading even to dismissal.

Giving Notice

How much notice is proper? Probably a month at the minimum, or the time it will take to complete a major project on which you are working. Hastier departures can leave your former employer in the lurch and that can tarnish your references there. While you are plotting your exit date, you should also be prepared to leave at the end of your notice interview. That means putting your office in order, removing what personal items you have there, and returning to the office any business items—books, papers, reports, equipment and anything else you have borrowed or taken home to work on.

Asking you to leave on the spot may seem like a harsh response from your employer but in some competitive situations or where something such as national security is involved, your presence, particularly if you are joining a direct competitor, may be deemed inappropriate. You have, in essence, broken a trust or a contract. But most often, you will find your departure regretted and you will be treated to a farewell luncheon or two and some cordial wishes for good luck. Just bear in mind that you might not, and plan for that contingency.

Be cooperative.

If it is possible, be willing to work with your successor or with staff to ensure a smooth transition. If it is appropriate, make yourself available on an informal, off-hours basis after you leave in case your old company has questions about your projects.

Remember references.

Now is also the time to check your references with a call or visit. In Chapter 6 you will find guidelines for selecting references that keep your job hunt confidential and your references called upon only when needed.

Bargain With a Job Offer?

What if you really want to stay, but you have a tempting offer? Circumstances vary, but bargain with a job offer only if you are willing to leave. You may be a valued employee and your company may make a generous counteroffer to keep you on board. You may find your boss willing to confess you were underpaid or your skills wasted on lower-level jobs. You may find yourself a notch or two higher on the organization chart, your prestige heightened. But you've also signaled that you were looking and you were willing to be courted. That's true even if you got the call when you weren't even looking. Bargaining with an offer from another company gets pegged as the crudest of tactics. Stay after such a bargain and you'll likely be gone in a year or two anyway.

Making Sure You're on the Right Track

With your mind more focused on your career than it may have been in years, this is the moment to look not just at what you do, but what you *could* do. This is the time to consider alternatives, as well—before you launch a full-scale job hunt, before you give notice, before you make crucial life-course decisions.

An alternative doesn't necessarily mean parting with your current employer. It can mean entering a training program for a new position or enhancing your present credentials with cross training in a foreign language, for example. In a year or two of night and weekend courses you can prepare yourself for a shift, or give your career a shot in the arm. Your company may even pay for your training.

But there may be a small voice in the back of your mind raising profound doubts about the course of your work life. The voice may have been there, but it was smothered by 12-hour work days, the threat of failure and the need to pay the mortgage. Now, you hear the voice, and if you're out of work, you've got time to listen. The message may be cloudy—only that you need answers to your questions, an objective assessment of who you really are. Or you may have a more developed concept of what *else* you want to do. The classroom may beckon. You may want the chance to learn a new profession, or simply the time to cool down in the one you have and see it from the perspective of a teacher. This chapter (as indeed is this book) is about the road not taken—at least not the first time—but one you may wander down today.

Vocational Testing

Some people knew from the beginning what they wanted to do. Dad was a doctor; Mom taught school. By gender, the kids picked their lifework and kept whatever unhappiness they felt to themselves. Today, we aren't so passive. When we're unsatisfied with our work, and simply shifting to another similar assignment seems pointless, then we want choices, alternatives. But they have to match our skills and interests. "What skills and interests?" you ask. After all, you're unhappy, or unemployed, so the old skills and interests don't seem useful.

They still are, as are a host of others you may not be aware of, that are waiting to be discovered. At least that's the promise

"I'm sorry you only lasted two days. Tell you what — I'll write on your reference that you did a cameo performance with us."

Reprinted by permission: Tribune Media Services

of vocational testing. Like most psychological testing, this form has its critics who argue among others things that certain of the tests don't measure the right criteria. Others think the work environment, with all its quirks and unique conditions, defies quantitative measurement. Besides, critics add, the tests don't take into consideration those environmental factors that can ruin even a good job—things like a long commute or a lousy office.

Testing's defenders say the tests, while not the end-all of vocational questions, can fill in important blanks.

Other critics say the tests aren't revised often enough to reflect occupational changes that occur over time. Some, for example, were devised before the huge influx of women into the job market.

Perhaps the most interesting criticism comes from Jeffrey Goldberg, president and chief psychologist of the Personnel Sciences Center in New York City. Dr. Goldberg thinks some people, ready to chuck a career and use the tests to find another, really need only to find a different niche in their own field.

Nevertheless, when you're groping for answers, apparently some information is better than no information because each year thousands of people take one of the major vocational tests to find out what they really should be doing.

Indeed, testing's defenders say the tests, while not the end-all of vocational questions, can fill in important blanks.

"Testing is one piece of the puzzle," says Robert Urie, former president of the International Association of Counseling Services. It accredits university, college, community college, private and public counseling agencies.

Testing can also help organize the pieces of that puzzle and give people a clearer picture of their interests and goals, says Lee Richmond, past president of the National Career Development Association.

Many Types of Tests

You'll find dozens of vocational-interest tests offered by everyone from college counseling offices to private aptitude-testing services and employers. Questions are either multiple choice, true or false, categorical (you like, dislike or are indifferent to something) or preferential (you say whether you'd rather talk to a few people at a party or everyone).

What's being measured are your abilities and interests in a variety of areas such as music, art, writing, mechanical skills, design, and so on. Some tests measure your aptitude for recognizing differences in various designs and shapes or how well you can remember a series of numbers or names.

In one dexterity test you move tiny pins from holes on one side of a board to holes on the other side. Another clocks you while you assemble something called a wiggly block, a piece of wood cut into wavy shapes.

Some counselors may have you take several tests as well as some measures of your personality in order to gain a more complete picture of your interests and skills.

There are three broad categories of vocational tests:

Interests

Here you choose likes and dislikes. Many tests look for what are called categorical consistents, which tabulate patterns in your responses according to categories of interests such as music or natural science. In other tests, your answers will be compared to those of lawyers or doctors who say they are happy with their work. In this category you'll find tests such as the Career Assessment Inventory and the Strong Interest Inventory. Both tests take a broad range of professions into consideration.

Aptitude

Tests in this area take several approaches to find answers. Some measure your performance in a specific job, such as computer programming or auto mechanics. Others reverse the process and look at what spatial skills or numerical talents you may have. A person good at visualizing structures, for example, would have an advantage in engineering, architecture or interior design.

Among popular aptitude tests are the Differential Aptitude Test Battery and the Johnson O'Connor Research Foundation's tests.

Still another variation more closely resembles intelligence tests, measuring how adept you are in such things as problem solving, or professional judgment. Here you'll find tests such as the Wide Range Achievement Test, Wonderlic Personnel Test, Nelson-Denny Reading Test and the Watson-Glaser Critical Thinking Appraisal.

Personality

These tests reveal how you work with others, your attitudes and your needs. The tests ask such questions as: Are

*Be sure you
understand what
the whole counseling
package includes
and costs.*

you ordinarily a highly social person or withdrawn? When you make decisions, do you show decisive action or do you procrastinate as long as possible? Your responses are matched to occupational profiles. If the test indicates that you are extroverted, then you might choose sales or teaching.

Among the most popular personality tests are the Myers-Briggs Type Indicator, the 16 PF, and the California Psychological Inventory.

Where to Go

You can take vocational tests in a number of places and spend anywhere from a nominal fee of $5 or $10 to $1,000 or more. Generally, public places such as college counseling offices charge less, while private counselors such as Johnson O'Connor, based in New York City, charge more.

- **You can find information on vocational testing in the Yellow Pages** under that heading or "Vocational Counseling," "Career or Job Counselors," or "Employment Counselors."

- **Also determine whether the agency you are considering is accredited by a national organization.** The National Board of Certified Counselors offers specialty certification for career counselors. For a list, contact NBCC, 3D Terrace Way, Greensboro, NC 27403.

- **For a list of locations of the well-regarded John C. Crystal Centers,** write The Crystal-Barkley Corp., 152 Madison Ave., 23rd Floor, New York, NY 10016. The centers offer lectures from experts in career change and from entrepreneurs as well as a list of successful career changers. Crystal-Barkley also has a software program you can use at home to do your own career testing.

Before you sign up for any tests, talk to friends and coworkers about any vocational tests they have taken. Set up a preliminary consultation before you agree to any counseling. You want to be sure you are compatible with the counselor.

Be sure you understand how much time the tests and counseling will take, what you will be charged and how many follow-up sessions and other services you will receive, such as help writing your resume.

You should be able to choose among the services, and if you terminate the counseling be charged only for those services you have received. Sessions should last about two days, not including interpretation of the tests.

What Does It All Mean?

Interpretation, on the other hand, should take at least several hours as you discuss the results and their meaning for you. You can ask to review those sections you do not understand and ask for additional sessions if you are still unclear about the meaning. This is, after all, the reason you began the process.

At the same time, you can't expect a religious conversion from this experience. While vocational tests are most often grounded in academic research, they shouldn't be construed as the definitive word on what you should do with your life work. It may be your discontent can better be dealt with through psychotherapy or other psychological counseling. Consider making any vocational tests you take part of a larger program of reassessment that includes looking at how you live—exercise, diet, and so on, where you live, your age and your beliefs.

Some counseling may also include help with reference sources on new careers suggested by the tests. The U.S. Government publishes its *Occupational Outlook Handbook* that is updated periodically and lists descriptions on more than 250 different occupations. Your local library can also help find other books that describe vocations, working conditions, pay and employment outlook. Chapter 8 includes information on researching companies that can be helpful to you at this time.

Go Back to School?

Your search for alternatives may lead you beyond vocational testing and into the classroom. You may see school as your ticket to a new career, one that has always interested

continued on page 79

John Frazier: Back to School

John Frazier was 39 years old when he decided to quit work as a developer of nursing homes and go back to school. "I love school," he says. "I love to take tests and it had always been in the back of my mind to get either a law degree or a medical degree. I can't stand the sight of blood, so the final choice was easy."

A native Texan, Frazier pulled up stakes in Washington, D.C. and in 1991 headed to the University of Houston. He wasn't alone on campus, about a third of all law students are beyond the early to mid twenties age of traditional law students. He says his age didn't appear to be a factor in his admissions. "My background in business helped, and it was a public school. I think a private school like Yale or Harvard might not have admitted me."

The rigors of first-year law took their toll, however. "It was unbelievable the first semester," he explains. "If you weren't in class you were studying, Sundays included," he says. "The second semester it was still 12 hours a day. It was hard, especially because I'd been out of an academic setting so long."

With a scholarship that paid tuition and gave him a stipend of $2,500 a year, Frazier had to tap less of his savings than the average student. Tuition and expenses at public law schools averages $10,000; at private schools it can run to $25,000.

He rented a house and lived modestly, working one summer as a law student intern for about $10,000 a season. "I didn't think about the lost income (of close to six figures annually)," he says. "It'll take me five years to make it up. But I will always be able to find a job where I can make some money."

When he graduated in 1994, Frazier scored in the top five per cent of his class, a critical move for getting offers. He had also served on the law review, another way to raise his profile. He did, however, feel the sting of his age when he went looking for legal work in his specialty of real estate law. "I was recruited somewhat, but not as much as others, and this is where my age hurt. The big firms have a notion of what you should look like."

He accepted an offer from Kelly, Hart & Hallman, a Fort Worth law firm with strong ties to the Bass family. His starting salary package was $63,500, which is above the average starting offer of $45,000. "It's a set rate of pay the first year. You go in as a first-year attorney no matter what your age."

His pay has risen since and he's actively involved in many of the firm's important cases. "The firm's partners treat you like a first year because you are," he explains. "But I have a lot of client contact and I've gotten bigger projects because I was older. Clients never ask what year you are—outside I wasn't a 'first year.'"

you. Your second chance at anything from horticulture to law or even medicine. You may decide this is the time to add extra skills to your background. Cross training in languages, for example, can be a powerful way to boost your career in time of falling political barriers and increasing international trade.

You may return to the classroom as a teacher, using your time to write about your profession or begin research on a facet of it that has captured your interest. You can use a term or two or more of teaching to sharpen your professional skills, distilling what you have learned to make a clearer picture in your own mind of what you want if and when you return to your profession.

You can use teaching as a way to meet leaders in your field or to raise your own profile among your peers as you publish papers and books that gain notice. (A full discussion of ways to move into teaching begins on page 83.)

It's easy to understand the allure of school if you just take a September morning, add the smell of old books and musty classrooms, the sound of a football scrimmage and the sight of a pair of young students holding hands. Chances are if more than a decade has passed since you were in school that should be a romantic enough notion to put you in the mood, especially if you're thinking of changing careers. You're young, barely middle-aged perhaps; there's at least a solid couple of decades ahead of you to build a new life doing something fresh and invigorating. The change is going to do you good.

Measuring the Financial Gain—or Drain

It might do you in, too. Going back to school *full-time* is expensive, even on a scholarship, even if some of the money's coming from a severance package, too. You'll step out of the income stream for at least a year, maybe three or more. That money is gone, at least for the foreseeable future, and unless you were really underpaid, or you are headed for a very fast track when you finish the coursework, you aren't going to make it back any time soon. More likely, if you are changing careers, you'll see your income fall by as

Unless you were really underpaid, or you are headed for a very fast track when you finish school, you aren't going to make the money back soon.

Your experience is going to count more than almost any degree you could get.

much as half because you'll be starting near the bottom pay rungs. Be sure you understand how dramatic a change you are proposing to your lifestyle and ask yourself how much of a risk taker you really are.

Unless you're going after a professional degree necessary to practice law, medicine or teaching, your experience is going to count more than almost any degree you could get. Even if you want to teach, you can probably wangle a position based on your background and pick up the additional coursework or any advanced degrees you will need to stay on *while* you teach. And you can cut the financial drain by earning a degree part-time and staying on the job.

That's not to say you measure a return to campus solely for its financial reward, but if you have a family, or children facing their own collegiate days, you probably should consider the financial ramifications.

Is it worth it? That's the question a Harvard survey asked its School of Government mid-career program graduates. The students, all of whom had at least five years of work behind them, listed personal growth as the most important (95% of the respondents) reward of their time in the one-year program. 95 percent said they learned important skills and knowledge and 78% believed the degree helped increase their employment value. How much? The survey said the average graduate (who was 36) picked up a 16% pay raise over a pre-Harvard salary.

The study paints a relatively positive picture of school. About half of the Harvard class came from government and returned to government, so theirs was more of a take-charge maneuver than seeking alternatives. Still, 91% said they would do it again and on average, they rated their job satisfaction after taking the courses as 7 when the scale is 1 to 9. That's a contented group of bureaucrats who took time out of their careers for a year of graduate school and were happy they did. If that's your position, or at least your attitude, you may be as fortunate.

Getting In

With so many adult students taking courses, you should be welcomed at your local college or university. If you're taking a short course, such as a five-day program for training real estate agents, you'll probably be dealing with the college's extension service, its division for short-term adult studies. Entrance standards there will be essentially open to anyone with an interest. These abbreviated courses can also enhance your standing within your present company or make a transfer easier to achieve.

If you enter a formal degree program, you'll be judged by the same standards as any student. You may have to take pre-entrance exams such as the Graduate Record Examination. You may also have to take makeup courses to qualify yourself for professional school. That happened to Pamela Thayer, who loved animals but worked as a speech pathologist in the Virginia public school system. After nine years of teaching she decided to go to back to college and become a veterinarian. She applied to the Virginia-Maryland Regional College of Veterinary Medicine, in Blacksburg, Va. Turned down the first time for lack of science training, she spent the next two years making up the deficit at a community college. Once accepted, she spent four years and more than $45,000 to become a vet.

Thayer found the return emotionally taxing, and the competition strenuous. But she graduated, and took a job as a vet in Elkton, Md., matching her old salary with the promise of a higher salary once she established a practice. She later moved to Bealton, Va., after marrying a fellow veterinarian, and is now earning more than she did as a teacher. "The best surprise," she says of the change, "is not being bored when I go to work."

Getting Focused

Unlike your undergraduate days, if you're returning to campus to enroll in a full-time graduate program, you won't have the luxury of fishing through several majors before you find something you like. Unless you've got a corporate spon-

You may also have to take makeup courses to qualify yourself for professional school.

The gap between your generation and those around you may show as you attempt to explain Linda Ronstadt, My Lai or the sound of an Austin Healey's muffler before emission laws.

sor or a scholarship, it's truly your dime, but more importantly, it is your time, so you shouldn't cross campus without a clear idea of what you want to study. Your vocational tests or meetings with the college's career-counseling staff can help you clarify those interests.

If you want to be clever about this and you have a genuine interest in languages, consider a master's in one of them. Be very clever and you'll pick Japanese or Chinese, two of the hottest "international business" languages today. Slavic languages may hold value as Eastern Europe develops. Spanish is perhaps the most versatile foreign language you can learn because so many U.S. immigrants speak that language. With that you could teach (in a warmer climate such as Miami, for instance), or work with a firm doing business in Central or South America or in Spain, for example. Many companies are creating offshore operations where labor is cheaper. U.S. bank check processing, for example, is done in some Caribbean countries, with the records flown back and forth on overnight flights.

Life as an Older Student

Once you're in, you may need refresher courses or even tutors to help you gear up for academia. Thinking as a student may require some adjustment. Term papers and a thesis or doctorate can be major projects requiring sophisticated research skills. If your course outline doesn't include basic research methods, consider taking courses in that discipline.

You'll be among fresh-faced and often sharp students who could be half your age but have twice the background knowledge you have, especially if you are shifting careers. Your war stories, however entertaining, won't always be appreciated, either by students full of their own ideas or professors threatened with losing center stage.

The gap between your generation and those around you may show as you attempt to explain Linda Ronstadt, My Lai or the sound of an Austin Healey's muffler before emission laws. If you ship off for grad school in another city, you may end up in a dormitory, reliving those thrilling days of underdone chicken and overcooked eggs. Get cooped up in a 9-by-12 bedroom stripped of your usual comforts, and you may suffer depression or shock.

You may smile at this, but it is a real consideration for anyone settled into a job and a house and career. You'll be chucking all that for an extended period at a time when you'll be under stress in a strange environment and where money may also be short. School is invigorating, but be sure you've graded all the factors before you go.

Another Kind of School

Don't take too seriously the axiom that "Those who can't do, teach." Shaw was wrong. For you, teaching may be the time you need to recharge batteries and set a new course in your career—or to discover you thrive in a classroom.

You can choose either the college level or the high school level, depending on your interests and skills. If you're still in your present job, you can start with an evening or weekend course at a local college, or perhaps a class for adults seeking a high-school equivalency degree. If you've left work, you can try it full-time or teach a few courses and either take some yourself in fields you want to explore or use the free time for other activities—that book you've wanted to write, or the business you want to start. You will have some income, perhaps even enough to live as you had been. And you will have time to consider what you want to do next.

If you seek a higher level, you'll find fertile opportunities in colleges and universities. You can start with as loose an arrangement as being an adjunct teacher on the faculty, teaching specified classes for a specified fee. The position has its drawbacks. You don't enjoy all the "rights and privileges" of ordinary faculty—you're not on tenure track, for example, and you probably won't receive any benefits beyond access to the faculty lounge.

If you want something more substantial, you may be able to join the faculty as a lecturer, a junior position without the status of a professorship, but generally you're on the payroll drawing benefits. If your former position carries enough weight within the academic community, you may find yourself working as an assistant professor with an academic future.

Teaching may be the time you need to recharge batteries and set a new course — or to discover you thrive in a classroom.

Forty-one states and the District of Columbia now offer alternative teaching certificate programs.

Much depends on the discipline in which you are working—writing, for instance, offers more latitude than astrophysics.

Community colleges, with an orientation toward vocations and plenty of older students, may offer you more opportunity. Most times you won't need a doctorate should you want to make your arrangements long term.

A shortage of high school math and science teachers spawned innovative programs that capitalize on your skills and knowledge in those fields and allow you to teach with less preparation than is offered in traditional teacher accreditation programs.

More than forty states and the District of Columbia now offer alternative teaching certificate programs and more than 50,000 teachers have been licensed since 1986. Generally, the requirements are that the person hold an undergraduate degree, often in the field in which they are teaching. Rebecca Goben, a teacher in the Houston school system, had to take evening training classes and 12 hours of education to complete the alternative teacher program several years ago. The former banking official had tired of her career after eight years and found teaching the perfect alternative. The $6,000 pay cut she took that first year "was a shockeroo," but she's made that up and more since. She also overcame the prejudice of traditionally-trained teachers who questioned her competence the first year she taught. Since then she's become part of a corps of Houston alternative teachers whose record is so strong, that new alternative applicants at one point accounted for more than half the teachers hired in the Houston district. Goben is so happy she's since earned a master's degree and can see herself teaching at the college level someday.

Be Your Own Boss

You could really scare yourself and start a business. You wouldn't be an American in the 1990s if you didn't think about dumping the 9-to-5 routine and making a go of it on your own. America grew on the strength of private, and often small, enterprise. Restlessness fueled by a near reckless willingness to do it ourselves has sent millions of us into our own businesses. When luck and skill teamed with good timing, giants such as Ford Motors and IBM grew from those beginnings. The mere thought of that keeps many an entrepreneur on duty long into the night.

Of course, you remember the big successes. But most people's experience with their own business isn't that way at all. Strike out on your own and that's what you're likely to do—strike out. Self-employment is fraught with risk: Four out of five new businesses fail within five years (although that number may be too pessimistic. According to Dun & Bradstreet, looking at real businesses, ones that purchase supplies and sell products or services, shows a better survival rate. Two thirds of those businesses are still in existence several years after they are founded.)

Balderdash, you say, and the facts give your voice some conviction. More than 625,000 new businesses are started each year. These entrepreneurs found cash from their own reserves, family, and financial institutions.

Figures such as that make a strong argument for giving your thoughts of starting a business a shot. And if you're serious enough to be looking for another position, or staring at a termination date where you are, then you have an even more powerful reason—or fewer excuses not—to look into it.

Your business can be as small as just you, incorporated, working at home.

Don't leave out becoming a consultant, a course of action that leaves you in the same game, just playing a different position. You'd be your own boss, but you wouldn't be saddled with much of the paraphernalia you'd require to set up and run other businesses. At least at first, you could operate out of your own home, might not need financing, and wouldn't have to worry about incorporating, for example. Of course, there are other considerations, which are described beginning on page 100.

A single chapter in this book can't tell you everything you will need to know in order to start a business, but it can provide you with a framework to use for considering that possibility and offer some sources for more information.

If you decide to try your own business, you'll be joining a burgeoning group of entrepreneurs who are riding the crest of a substantial movement in this country. In 1970, says James Challenger, the outplacement-firm executive, maybe one in ten of his clients tried their own business. Most instead sought re-employment in their field. Today, one in five makes a go of it on their own. Your *business* can be as small as just you, incorporated, working at home. A study by Link Resources, a New York City firm that monitors the communications technology market, found that in 1996 some 9.6 million telecommuters worked from home part or full-time during normal business hours. In 1989, five million had done that in a single year.

Now Is a Great Time

What changed? The way we do business, for one thing. As a greater segment of the work force moves into services, we learn that those services, unlike much manufacturing, can be performed outside of the office—and even from home. For example, the computers that at first kept your branch office linked with the headquarters in Phoenix can now keep you linked from home to the branch office. Add car phones and fax machines and you see that the structure is in place for this exodus from the office.

Other factors may have been at work, too. The first of

the "boomer" generation born after World War II is reaching middle age and showing a fondness for staying at home. Dubbed *cocooning*, this makes a home office all the more compelling, especially when the likes of computers and modems can keep a homebound person in instantaneous touch with the office. International competition blurs time, stretching the "workday" around the clock so that calling from home is required to keep up with events.

Big corporations have latched onto these trends as a way to keep down costs. A host of formerly in-house functions such as payroll, mail delivery and housekeeping have already been largely turned over to outside suppliers. And they're being joined by increasingly sophisticated functions such as employee relations and even project management, using former executives familiar with a company's goals and procedures.

Harris, Cartoonists & Writers Syndicate

The process has grown to such proportions that some companies farm out nearly everything. Only a small staff of overall managers is on the payroll at these corporations, the rest of the work is done by contractors. The opportunities this has created for the small business person or the professional supplying services are enormous.

Your First Moves

Whether vocational testing pointed the way or you're thinking of launching a business on your own intuition, you'll need sound advice before you start. With so many start-up businesses failing within the first few years, it's probably going to take more than your mom's great cookie

Most entrepreneurs are inner directed, and their relentless pursuit is among their greatest assets.

recipe to succeed. It's critical to know if you're the kind of person who succeeds on you're own.

The Entrepreneurial Spirit

Before you go very far along the path toward your own business, consider these issues:

What does your family think?

This is a set-up question. The real question is, do you care what they think or what anyone else thinks? If you don't, take heart. While you should and must seek wise counsel for answers to many questions as you consider going out on your own, a persistent sense of purpose that prevails despite adversity, or opinion, is most often a good sign. That's because most entrepreneurs are inner directed. Despite what they may say, they don't care; their relentless pursuit is among their greatest assets.

Is it entrepreneurship that propels you or are you a manager yearning for more control?

A survey by the Center for Entrepreneurial Management found that successful entrepreneurs launched their own businesses because they didn't like working for someone else. Fired managers who were questioned said they would do it to make money. Entrepreneurs said customers, an idea and hard work were the top requirements to make a business go. Managers said cash was the key. The advice for you if you see yourself on the corporate side of this study: Take a partner or go into a joint venture with an established firm.

How committed are you?

Yes, we're hammering a theme here that you must really, truly want to do this or your chances of succeeding are severely reduced. Running your own business is going to take many hours of your time, with no guarantee that any of it will pay off. Any payoff you do receive can be slow in coming, building over the years until you finally have something to show for your work. Meanwhile, you'll be explaining yourself to your family and friends, who may not understand the slowness of your progress. Ignoring the financial considerations for the moment, can you endure what can be a slow erosion of faith in your idea by those around you?

Other Key Issues

Being of a mind to begin your own business isn't the only attribute of a successful entrepreneur. Other factors must be in place to raise your odds of success.

Who do you know?

Yes, it's that word again—network. If you think tapping it for job leads is its only value you are wrong. Tapping your network for aid in starting a business is very important. Your professional contacts can help you choose a business, shape a business plan and find employees. It can be a source of investment money, and a continuing place to garner advice. Hence, how good a network do you have? And who makes good network? Kay Gurtin of Chicago can answer those questions. She was a securities salesperson for several years in the 1980s. She did well, pulling down a six-figure salary in that high-pressure environment. Then, with the birth of her son, she was out of a job and searching for part-time work. Her solution was to tap her network of former colleagues and contacts for advice. They knew her, her skills, and the marketplace. She met with them often. Those meetings led to the creation of Executive Options, which places professionals like herself in part-time or temporary positions. Her voluntary board of executives helped her devise a business plan and met with her regularly to discuss possible refinements. "It's a huge credibility boost to have this board backing me," she says.

Are you healthy enough?

There are two issues here: First, are you physically up to the task? And, perhaps as critical an issue, can you qualify for affordable health insurance? Starting your own business is physically and mentally exhausting for many people. If you have high blood pressure, a weak heart or a chronic disease that saps your energy, you may find yourself out of business, or worse, before you're a success. If you can't get health insurance coverage, you'll be exposing your business, and your family, to undue risk.

What's your reputation?

Are you known as someone who keeps your word? Have you always paid your bills? Are you active in your community? Most money for businesses comes from the people who start them, from their friends and from local lending institutions. Your reputation will precede you in the market-

For More Information

You'll undoubtedly want help before you decide whether or not to go into business for yourself.

The SBA

The U.S. Small Business Administration has branch offices in many cities. You can find the one nearest you under U.S. Government in your telephone directory (or by calling 800–827–5722). Or write to headquarters at 409 3rd St., S.W., Washington, DC 20416. The SBA is also a source of start-up money, offering guaranteed loans up to $750,000.

When you contact the SBA, ask for the Resource Directory for Small Business Management. It lists scores of SBA booklets on topics for small business startup. Write: Office of Business Initiative, SBA, 409 3rd St., S.W., Washington, DC 20416.

The Center for Family Business

If you're considering starting a family business and you want help, write to the Center for Family Business (P.O. Box 24268,

Cleveland, OH 44124). The Center, established more than two decades ago, offers counseling to family businesses as well as educational information and consulting.

Books

Kiplinger's Working for Yourself, by Joseph Anthony (Kiplinger Books), offers a thorough look at all the issues you will encounter as you consider and set up a small business.

The Macmillan Small Business Handbook, by Mark Stevens, (Macmillan) is a comprehensive guide for would-be business owners and includes outlines for raising money, tax planning, and computerizing your business.

Growing Your Own Business, by Paul Hawken (Fireside), is more impressionistic, its strength lying in Hawken's discussions of his own experience founding a successful health food chain and the Smith & Hawken garden supply catalog company.

place; if it's even a bit tarnished, you may have a harder time making your business successful.

How good is your idea?

Successful entrepreneurs are known for their deep commitment to an idea. But to succeed it can't be just any idea. It's got to be a good idea, one with a chance for success based on solid market research, realistic goals and constant feedback from the marketplace. A hunch and intuition are often critical to the creation of an idea, but the successful execution means getting answers. Is there a market for your product or service? What's a fair price? Can you make a profit on that? Who is the competition?

To answer many of these questions, plan on some sessions at the library researching the business you want to enter. Look for books devoted specifically to your choice as well as those that look at broader topics such as franchising. An example of the former is *The Writing Business,* by the editors of *Coda: Poets and Writers Newsletter* (Pushcart Press; out of print; check your local library). For the latter, there is *Owning Your Own Franchise,* by Herbert Rust (Prentice Hall). The Bureau of Labor Statistics also publishes the *Occupational Outlook Handbook,* which outlines what it is like to work in a specific vocation. The book also predicts growth for different industries and lists sources for more information. In *Ben & Jerry's: The Inside Scoop* (Crown), author Fred "Chico" Lager, the famous ice cream makers' former chairman, outlines an inspiring story of how two guys built a small empire on high quality—to say nothing of high calorie—ice cream with wacky names and innovative ingredients.

Talk to people who are doing what you want to do. You'll find most of them willing to describe their businesses, sometimes in great detail. Spend time with them, or at least observe how they work. Visit as many places as you can find, considering as you do whether the market for your service or product might already be saturated. Check the *Encyclopedia of Associations* at your library for groups dealing with the business you're considering. These organizations often have material you can use and people to talk with about your plans.

Talk to people who are doing what you want to do. Watch them work.

Will you give your former employer a run for his money?

Related to your idea, although it may not apply to everyone is this: what's your old boss going to say? That is, are you taking trade secrets with you that you'll be barred from using? If you worked under an employment contract, check that, too, to be certain there is nothing blocking you from competing with your old employer if that's what you intend to do.

"Higgins, we've decided to let you go before you become irreplaceable."

From The Wall Street Journal, Permission, Cartoon Features Syndicate

Where will you find money for your business?

Undercapitalization kills as many companies as a bad idea. It is not unusual for businesses to remain unprofitable for two years or more before turning the corner. You will need enough capital to support your business and your living expenses. In the course of growing a business, you may need to liquidate assets such as a mutual fund, or investment property. You may tap the equity in your home. These are major decisions you cannot make alone if you have a family. You must create a business plan, as you'll see below. But you must also consult with those people who rely on you for support to be certain they agree to your plan.

You should talk with a representative of your bank. You may, in the course of establishing your business, need a loan or a line of credit you can tap when you need money. A banker can assess your financial condition and advise you on how much you could expect to receive in a loan, or how much credit the bank would be willing to make available to you as a small business person.

Talk with your lawyer and, if you have one, an accountant. You will have decisions to make regarding how you structure your business, report your income and expenses, and protect yourself from legal liability. You will also need advice on maintaining records, creating contracts and signing leases or other contracts for services you yourself need in the course of doing business. An accountant can help you with tax strategies to ensure that you get every self-employed tax break to which you are entitled.

Have you created a business plan?

A formal outline of what you want to do and how you propose to do it is important, whether or not you are going to use it to seek outside money for your business.

- **First, a business plan clarifies in your mind what you are doing,** providing you with a goal to work toward and an objective look at what you are proposing.

- **Second, it is an operating manual for you to use** once you are under way, detailing your spending and income and indicating whether or not you are on target with your projections.

- **Finally, it is a formal way to tell would-be investors what you want and why you are worthy of a loan.** You will almost invariably need a business plan, especially if you are dealing with lending institutions.

A typical plan describes your business—what you intend to do, your market, who will manage the business and what your competition is. A second section outlines your balance sheet, what you plan to spend for equipment, rent, and so on, an analysis of income and expenses that shows when you will break even, a cash-flow projection month-by-month for a year, and statements that show your financial worth at the beginning of the project.

In a third section you supply supporting documents such as your resume, letters of reference, credit reports and any other papers relevant to your business.

The Business Planning Guide, by David H. Bangs, (Upstart) and *The Small Business Handbook,* by Irving Burstiner (Fireside) are two good sources of outlines for a business plan.

Don't ignore a business plan once it is written or once it has brought you an infusion of money. It is your personal auditor, a way of measuring how you are doing and an important guide to keep you on track.

continued on page 95

Paula Coppel: Working For Herself—The Long-term Perspective

Paula Coppel tumbled through a series of writing and reporting jobs in the 14 years after graduating from the University of Illinois in 1977. By the time she started her own communications business in 1991 in Portland, Ore., she was looking for part-time work and a chance to try her hand at creative writing. But a divorce pushed security to the top of the priority list as she became the primary bread-winner for two young children.

Her business, writing speeches, articles and publications and planning communications strategy, went through the typical ups and downs of a new enterprise: The challenge of finding clients and doing the work as well as marketing the business. Added to that was the stress of being a single parent. "I knew I had to keep working to keep the money coming in," says Coppel, now in her early 40s. "That was when I most missed the security of a paycheck. Then there are all the financial changes, like having to buy your own health insurance. I also had to find ways to keep from being lonely."

She found another consultant to share office space. That eased some of the loneliness. A stable base of four steady clients who renewed their contracts reduced the insecurity of being self-employed.

Coppel soon had to cope with a problem many entrepreneurs hope to have. By the mid 1990s, five years of successful self employment left her feeling in a rut. "It felt like I was doing the same things over and over," she explains. For a time she considered rejoining a firm.

She rejected that idea once she realized she had options. "If you start feeling like you don't have them, then you are dying," she says. "I realized that this isn't the way it always has to be. I like to edit, and that's an undeveloped part of my business. So I am working on that, and on developing my planning and strategy business."

She's also again working on creative writing projects—the very thing that prompted her to start her own business but which had been dormant these past years.

The business too has proved it can self-rejuvenate. Coppel went five years without raising her rates until one client told her she should do so for credibility. She cranked them up on a client-by-client basis some 20%. She also pushed herself harder to get out and talk to people—the only kind of marketing she does. Talking to employees inside a corporate communications department has reminded her why she still likes working for herself.

"When you are working in a corporation, there is a pretty strong element of fear. Those people don't want to break the rules or get people mad at them. I feel sorry for people trapped in that stress. Once you're on your own, you have more risk, but you also have more freedom."

A Second Round of Decisions

You've got plenty of choices to make even after you decide what you want to do.

New business or old?

Will you start the business yourself or buy an existing one? Start one yourself and you will probably need less up-front money, but buy an existing business and you could incur less risk. Weigh your interests and finances in order to decide. For the true entrepreneur, the game is creation, not management, so starting a business is most attractive. But maybe you are a born salesperson, comfortable meeting and bartering with the public, able to accept rejection. You aren't interested in setting up systems or designing products, you just want to sell them. An existing business, especially a franchise, would probably suit you better.

What form should the business take?

Will you incorporate or make it a partnership or a sole proprietorship? A sole proprietorship or a partnership is simpler and cheaper to set up than a corporation and easier to dissolve. Bookkeeping is often simpler. Whatever you make from your business is reported on your personal tax return. The most significant drawback is that you are personally liable for debts and damages your business incurs. That means your house, car and personal savings are on the line. That's the principal reason many people choose to incorporate, either as a closely held corporation or as a *subchapter S* corporation. Under these arrangements, your company is liable, not you. It can file for bankruptcy and liquidate its assets without involving your home and personal possessions. The drawback of a corporation is that sometimes you end up paying taxes twice on the income, once from your corporation and a second time on the income you pay yourself.

Discuss all these options with your attorney, and have him or her review your papers and prepare your incorpora-

The most significant drawback to not incorporating is that you are personally liable for debts and damages your business incurs.

tion papers. *The Field Guide to Starting a Business,* by Stephen M. Pollan and Mark Levine (Fireside), is a good source of information on the legal procedures necessary to safeguard your fledgling business.

Are you covered?

You'll need several kinds of insurance.

- **First, you should have** *property loss* to cover you against fire, vandalism or other damage.

- **Second, you'll want** *liability insurance,* should someone be injured while in your shop, for example.

- **Then there is** *key-person loss,* which will pay you an amount if you are unable to work for a period of time.

- **Finally, there** is *business-interruption coverage,* which covers you if, as the name implies, business is interrupted by a fire or another disaster.

Your insurance agent can help you arrange for policies.

What if you succeed?

Most entrepreneurs never intend to sell. Many, however, make lousy managers of growing companies whose needs have changed, sometimes dramatically, as a result of success and growth. Experts in small-business creation suggest that early on you have a plan that provides for success. That should include consideration of how you'll add partners and investors should you want to enlarge beyond your cash flow, and name successors to your position.

Once you're committed to creating your own business, you should plan for how to value it should you be taken from the picture by illness or death, for example, or for tax and estate purposes. By extension of the argument, you'll also need a plan for the sale of your company. You'll want to decide how assets would be distributed, how your name would be connected with the firm and a host of related questions you probably haven't given a moment's thought.

One Couple's Experience

For Kevin Brannon and Marjorie McGinnis, the road to their own business started over a beer—and ironically, that's also where it ended up. The two met in a bar one afternoon in Martinsburg, W. Va. a few years ago. They fell in love, and Kevin, an attorney from Portland, Ore., decided this was also the moment to chuck his legal career and go into business for himself. Turns out beer was his hobby and so it was a microbrewery they set out to build.

It took them more than two years and three quarters of a million dollars to turn an empty warehouse in Frederick, Md., into the Frederick Brewing Company, makers of Blue Ridge Beer. It was a harrowing task that at times seemed destined to fail. But through it run the threads of every successful entrepreneurial adventure.

He picked something he liked.

Too many entrepreneurs grab at the first proposal they come across that looks like big money. Better to go after something you like, something you already understand. The nearly intuitive wisdom that follows can help you solve a myriad of problems that will cripple the ignorant. For example, Brannon had brewed beer in his basement since his college days. He patronized many of the microbreweries that dot the Portland area. He knew what he liked, and he understood how to make it. When it came time to develop the beers he would make, he knew exactly what kind of lager, porter and stout would sell.

He played to his strengths.

Sure he knew how to brew beer, but he wasn't going to attract big money on that skill alone. So very quickly he determined he would hire a brewmaster. He would instead capitalize on his strengths as an attorney with substantial experience in small business ventures and franchises. It was his training and experience as an attorney that convinced many investors to put their money in the project.

The nearly intuitive wisdom that comes with pursuing something you already like and understand can help you solve problems that will cripple the ignorant.

He wrote a thorough business plan.

Brannon spent six months developing what turned into a 32-page business plan and a 15-page report on financial projections. His business plan covered everything from his qualifications, to the state of the microbrewery business, how he would structure the deal for investors and how he would market the beer. He also planned for success, expansion and a new brewery within five years. Lawrence Allen, a local bank official, says the business plan was the key to granting Brannon and McGinnis a $200,000 loan.

He tapped two networks.

With McGinnis's help, Brannon tapped a network of experts who could help him find land, meet legal requirements, and line up investors. He found local investors through this network and tapped both again and again for advice and money.

They stayed at it.

Through thick and thin, Brannon and McGinnis hung in, living off savings and the proceeds from the sale of his house in Portland. "We said we would give it everything we had, seven days a week, night and day, for five years," says Brannon. It didn't take that long. The brewery was profitable in its first full month of operation in January 1994. Two years later, Brannon and McGinnis had outgrown their original facility and were financing a new brewery nearby. Their award-winning Blue Ridge Beer is available in much of the East. Brannon jokes that with success they've lightened the workload, now taking a couple of days a month off.

A Home-Based Business?

If you want to work at home, the results of a 1989 *Wall Street Journal* study are still worthy of your attention. It found that 49% of the people polled still felt the benefits of working at home were outweighed by the drawbacks. Chief among the latter:

- Not having enough supplies or equipment.

- Having too many family interruptions.

- Mixing work with family life too much.

- Being distracted by household chores.

- Not having interaction with co-workers.

- Not having a regular routine.

- Having trouble quitting after a full day.

- Feeling work is less important if done at home.

Still, there was a positive spin to the findings. Of those polled, 53% thought more control over their work schedule was the top attraction to working at home. Among the other benefits, ranked by popularity:

- Wearing more comfortable clothes.

- Avoiding a commute.

- Not having a boss close by.

- Being able to care for children.

- Not having interruptions from co-workers.

- Job seeming less like work.

- Not minding overtime as much.

Showing the downside, however, is a 1992 study by the Washington State Energy Office of 280 telecommuters working at home in the Puget Sound area. One third of them stopped working at home. The biggest reason: They lacked equipment. A nearly equal number cited problems at the office, which they felt resulted from their not being on site. Another reason? They just didn't enjoy it.

Setting up a home office is based, however, on more than a series of impressionistic responses to a questionnaire. You will need to decide on an array of factors before you start working at home. The first question is, "Can you do it legally?" Zoning laws and homeowner association rules may prohibit your business. If they don't, you'll have to deter-

If you're consulting, (like all self-employment) you're only as good as the last job. Stop hustling work and you're out of business.

mine if there is space in your home, if it can successfully be modified for your business and what that will cost, what kind of equipment you will need, and so on.

Consulting

There was a time not that long ago when consulting— offering advice or technical expertise in what are considered professional vocations—was little more than a euphemism for unemployment. Anyone who was consulting was killing time until a real, full-time job came along.

Not anymore. Too many companies are recognizing the worth of part-time, single-project professionals and too many successful consultants have put to rest that moniker. Today, consultants who hustle can routinely boast that they make more than they did when they worked for someone else (and often that someone is their former employer).

What's more, while the cash is rolling in, a good number of them are being offered full-time positions that they are routinely turning down. That's because the same network that got them the consulting job will yield job leads. And who knows better what a company is looking for than someone who has been working for it? Positioning isn't all to the advantage of the consultant, either. Employers get to see on-the-job performance by consultants, and there is no better way to assess a would-be employee than a job tryout. Indeed, it seems that one of the greatest challenges of consulting can be knowing when to say "no" to a job offer.

But consulting isn't all peaches and cream. It's a hustle. Like hunting for a job, you're the salesperson *and* the product. Like all self-employment, you're only as good as the last job. Stop hustling work and you're out of business. There are no sick days that don't come out of your hide, no sloughing off you won't ultimately pay for, no cutting off a half hour here or there for a little squash game. If you weren't a model employee before, turn to consulting and you will be or you won't be a consultant for long.

And if you thought networking was a nice idea, try living on it, not just scouting a job lead once in a while. You'll face another gut-wrenching challenge. That's dealing with the person who doesn't pay up. You won't be able to simply send the bill to accounts receivable. It'll be *your* problem. And there's a variation on the theme that will make you stay current on your own bills: the client or account that is routinely late and has to be hounded for payment. Many, many companies seem to have taken a position that until you threaten you don't have to be taken seriously.

Titles are vaporous memories. As a consultant, now you're the president of...you.

Measuring Your Odds

Experience is the biggest factor. You should have at least five years of solid work behind you before you consider going out on your own. You should have a network of contacts who would hire you, not just say nice things about you but pay you for your work. It's one thing to stand on your deck and expound on how you could help someone with their business and quite another to turn that into a contract.

Bridging the gap—being taken seriously by others in your profession—is the greatest challenge for many consultants. That is followed closely by the sense of loss that many newly-minted consultants feel when they leave a company and go out on their own. You will no longer be a member of a team. Nor will you be backed by the prestige and influence of a powerful corporation. Titles are vaporous memories. As a consultant, now you're the president of...*you.* Big deal, some say. They miss the real power that a title like *executive vice president* carried in the marketplace. Your corporate headquarters is your spare bedroom.

If you're considering consulting, measure the quality of your network carefully. Those names are your link to whatever success you will have. If you have the choice, you may want to stay on the job a bit longer while you strengthen your ties to these people (and polish your reputation where you are because your own ex-employer can be an important first client).

Three Prerequisites

If you can overcome the drawbacks that come with going out on your own, you'll still need three sets of skills, says Wheaton, Md. consultant and author Herman Holtz, to succeed as a consultant.

Something to sell

First, you have to have an expertise, a skill or knowledge of value in the marketplace. For example, there's little reason to hire a consultant whose business expertise is the making of polyester double knit. At least not right now. Unfortunately, one of the problems a redundant middle manager faces is that the market could be glutted with people sharing the same talent.

Beyond marketable expertise, some professions seem to lend themselves to consultancies more readily than others. In the 1990s, the vocations shown in the adjacent list are solid ground for consulting careers. What makes those categories appropriate is that each involves specific tasks that must be tailored to a particular situation. That means individual attention, often on site, and that's the perfect formula for any consultant seeking work. You can judge other opportunities with the same criteria as you sort through the possibilities for your own consulting career.

Sales ability

You must know how to market yourself, how to meet people, convince them that they need you and strike a deal for your services. This is where your network and your ability to exploit it come to bear, especially in the beginning, when you'll make cold calls as you look for business. As we noted earlier, this can be daunting to someone accustomed to working in the structured environment of a corporation where these tasks are given to specialists. "The best way to network for business," says Holtz, "is by developing your own visibility as an expert. Writing, speaking and networking, being prominent at conventions, this is how people get to know who you are. This is a word-of-mouth business."

Tolerance for rejection

Part of marketing yourself will be dealing with turndowns. You can't help but take it personally, at least at the start. You, after all, are the one being rejected. It's a double punch, too, in that you will be pushing a product very important to you—yourself and your idea for doing something. It's a tough mindset to attain where you can back an idea—a proposal or the like—to the hilt, yet be able to walk away from it if it is rejected. (Although in time, you may discover that some of your bright ideas had more life than you expected and will come alive another day, making this process all the more complex.)

The bottom line is you will become a hawk with regard to spending.

An eye on the bottom line

Finally, you have to be able to manage your business. That means getting the work out, billing for it, keeping your books, paying your taxes and keeping the whole enterprise organized and afloat. Here you'll learn why consultants have to charge what seems to be a lot of money for their services—say $600 or $800 a day. For one thing, nobody works every day. Some weeks you'll be alone with your thoughts, with no one asking for your services.

You've also got expenses such as computers, telephone lines and answering machines, perhaps a secretary or an assistant. You have professional memberships, conferences to attend, luncheons to host. The bottom line is you will become a hawk with regard to spending, keeping copious records of your time and expenses. If not, you'll pay someone else to sort out the mess.

You May or May Not Succeed

Consultants come and go. But you'll be connected to your profession, or exploring a new one, and your network of professional contacts will grow. So if you get tired, or feel you're not as successful as you want to be, you'll be in an excellent position to step back into corporate employment. You may consider joining a consulting firm, a hybrid that offers you the stability of a company with the freedom to move from assignment to assignment. In the meantime, you've experienced the satisfaction of being your own boss.

The Search for a New Job

It's understandable: You recognize the first real sign of discontent or see the writing on the wall and realize your job may be on the line. You mail a hastily prepared resume, or make a couple of calls all but begging your friends for a job.

Those are the wrong moves, especially for someone with your skills and talents. A successful job hunt for someone at mid-career is dicier than for new pups. Employers will judge you on so many more variables—your record and judgment, how you developed your skills and which ones you developed further. Too many mid-career job seekers take antiquated skills into the marketplace and get blown away by people no more qualified except that they kept up. Add to that a substantial salary and rusty job-hunting skills. Competition will be fierce, and you must do better.

Section Two will help you prepare for and carry through your mid-career job search. You'll learn how to:

- get yourself in shape for the hunt,
- tap your network, the best source of job offers,
- write a resume that gets you an interview,
- handle headhunters, and
- succeed in an interview, even a tough one, to ensure you're still in the running, not out on the street.

It's a Job to Get a Job

Thisis a pep talk, a little basic training, rehearsal for your next task, looking for work. It's here because the moment you begin your search, you're on. You only make a first impression once. Ruin that chance, and you'll always be arguing from a weakened position. So this chapter will ensure you don't make mistakes even before you've started.

Looking for work is work. Your search can and should take all of a workday to accomplish. If you're still on the job, you're facing a double shift of sorts as you conduct your business and your current employer's business. If you are no longer employed, it is still a full-time job. But no less challenging, as anyone who has ever hunted for a job at this time can tell you.

- You do it on lunch hours and at the edges of the day, evenings and weekends.

- You take personal leave for interviews.

- You have all correspondence sent to your home.

- You limit calls to your office as much as possible.

- You give out your work number only with the proviso that you really don't want to be contacted there unless it is unavoidable.

To protect your position, you must remain pure as driven snow. Get caught looking for a job and you may

As you network, remain cautious, offering the same positive reasons for your search as you would give in an interview.

need a new job more quickly than you had planned. Most companies, whether they will admit it or not, regard a job-hunting employee—even one responding to a recruiter who initiates the contact—as an outsider. You've declared yourself disloyal in their eyes. You could be cut off from decision-making meetings, left out of future planning and eliminated from the promotion list. Any chance you could change your mind and decide to stay gets forfeited. All this, and you may not find another job you want anyway.

Don't talk to people at work about your plans, or how you're doing. Loose lips sink more than ships. Don't start using up your sick days. Human resources offices are on to that, as are most managers. Keep at your job with your typical zeal for the work. Keep a straight face and deny everything you can.

As you network, remain cautious, offering the same positive reasons for your search as you would give in an interview (see Chapter 11). After all, your search may take months, you may decide to terminate it or postpone it because conditions have changed. Perhaps your goals have shifted or you have family or personal matters that make moving impractical or impossible. What a manager doesn't know won't hurt her in this regard.

Getting Organized

Whether you're still going to the office every day or are on your own, you've got plenty to do, even from the start.

A workplace

You'll need a place to conduct your business. (Remember, if you're still working you don't want to leave evidence of your search at the office.) That can be your home office or a room you designate for the task while you find your new position. There you'll have a phone, an answering machine, a desk, a word processor or a high-quality electronic typewriter to prepare letters and resumes and a file cabinet for your records.

A business phone

If you're working full-time at finding a new job, a separate telephone line dedicated to your search is probably a good idea. You can answer this line professionally, just as you did at the office. It's not for your kids and it shouldn't be given out as an alternative number for any other purpose. It's the line prospective employers will call and hear you answer. It will be listed on your stationery and your resume as your office number.

A business address

To aid you as much as your image, give your home office a suite number. "Suite 200," for example, sounds businesslike, giving any home address a corporate look. It will also make your home office seem legitimate, and, by extension, the work you do in it.

Stationery

You'll need to order stationery (more on the weight and color in Chapter 7) now. You can find it in many office-supply companies and by mail order. Stock typefaces are fine, and stick to conservative designs.

Getting the Job Done

There's no rest for the job seeker. Rise and dress for this new work as you did for your last job. And keep regular business hours. The reasons for this are twofold. First, your morale and your self-esteem may have taken a beating if you left your old job against your wishes. You don't need to fan the fires of doubt by looking unemployed, and by definition, failed. You aren't going to act unemployed either. Sitting around in your bathrobe memorizing soap opera storylines is a sure way to oblivion if you wanted to be at work instead but didn't take your job-hunting time seriously. So, take a page from basic training. Rise and shine on time, every day, and go to your new office.

Second, this *isn't* a hollow charade in self deception. Once you're in that little room you do have things to accomplish.

Rise and dress for this new work as you did for your last job. And keep regular business hours.

Plan to have lunch with someone as often as you can to stay in circulation.

Make calls first.

Start in the morning with calls to members of your network, recruits for your network, names of people you've garnered already whom you want to contact for interviews.

You call in the morning to get in line. Most busy executives get plenty of calls in a day, and many return but a fraction of them. Often they call those they do not know who are most persistent. So call and call again, if you must, even if you find yourself recalling those thrilling days of yesteryear when you had a big company's name after yours and you were used to having your calls returned promptly. For now, accept that you may have to play a more patient game. Calling in the morning, even a bit before regular hours to catch executives before their phones are ringing off the hook, serves that purpose. You've got the day to try again, but you're catching people before the day's activities tie them up. If you're working, you'll use lunch hours and the end of the day as more time to make and receive calls. (For more on scheduling interviews, see Chapter 11.)

Do lunch.

Whether you're still at your old job or spending full-time looking for your next one, plan to have lunch with someone as often as you can. It's been part of your work pattern, for one thing. For another, it keeps you in circulation and up on the news of your business. And it is networking. Pick brains at lunch. Ask plenty of questions about other firm's activities. Get names and titles and telephone numbers.

Keep records.

Make careful, dated, notes of every telephone conversation, luncheon meeting and interview you have. Open a file—electronic or paper—for each person and company you have contact with. Type your notes if you can't read your own handwriting. Time may pass before you see these notes again, and you may forget the gist of the information you're placing on paper. Also place in the paper file any printed information you gather about companies you research.

What do you record? Any information pertinent to job openings, of course. But when you talk to people, make note of their interests, committees they serve on, outside activities, hobbies they mention, vacations they recall. If these people aren't in your network already, they ought to be. And networking is linking. You link something you've just learned about Cancun with someone who always intended to vacation there. You don't have to be crass about it: "Lynn, you owe me one." Just thoughtful: "Lynn, I bet you'd be interested in this."

Describe what you saw when you visited offices, what people told you about how the company does business, rewards achievement, responds to failure.

"We're looking for someone who's not afraid to take a risk and fall on his face."

Toos, Cartoonists & Writers Syndicate

All through this process you'll be sizing up a company's culture. You may have to work in it, so take advantage of every opportunity to measure it (more on culture in Chapter 8).

These notes are also useful at tax time. Much of what you spend on a job hunt will likely be deductible. But you will need records to keep track and to support your claim. Keep receipts, record mileage on your car and the like.

References

As you begin your search, contact those people you want to use as your references. They're your witnesses, if you will, willing to give testimony to your abilities. Before you release their names to any potential employer, talk with them. It's a courtesy, for one thing, to make sure they are available and willing to speak on your behalf. It is also an opportunity to make certain they are still good references. Talk to them about what they might say about you. Don't hesitate to remind them of your achievements or update them on what you've been doing. The fresher their acquaintance with your work, the more effective their reference will be.

At the same time, listen carefully to how they are responding to you. Has their attitude towards you changed? Are they reluctant references? It can be tough to confront someone you sense is reluctant, but remember, a bum reference, or even a lukewarm recommendation from someone whose name *you supplied* hits you twice. It's a bad reference, and it shows you didn't do your homework or perceive that you had a problem.

References fall into two categories, those you pick and those you have to give. The former are trusted friends, colleagues and supervisors who can speak personally on your behalf. They like you and respect your work. The second category are those people who categorically have an

Steve Brorsen: The Value of Persistence

How hard do you push to get a job? Harder than you may think. Steve Brorsen's example may be an extreme, but then he has a dream job at the Monterey Aquarium in Monterey, Cal. to show for it, so he thinks every year he spent working to get the job was worth it.

Brorsen loves fish, and natural sciences and aquatic life. But he studied psychology in college and had never worked in a public aquarium, so he knew getting a job at the Monterey Aquarium, which can pick from scores of candidates with doctorates in marine science, would be daunting. It was. He began his hunt for a job there with a resume and a fast rejection.

He returned two years later, arguing that he owned half a dozen aquariums at home and managed a pet shop in Monterey. Another turndown. This time he volunteered as a guide and animal caretaker, learning as much as he could about the fish,

crustacean and plant life that the aquarium draws from the bay and the Pacific Ocean.

He did that for two years and still was not offered work. Finally, he finagled a big newspaper feature story on his home aquariums and his love of fish.

The splashy story turned the tide and in 1988 he joined the aquarium staff. Today he maintains exhibits, collects new marine life for the aquarium and recently cared for a 230-lb. green sea turtle. On a given day he's out fishing in the bay, or gathering wildlife in the hills surrounding Monterey. He's been to Baja on expeditions and scuba diving for plant life.

"This is a coveted position," Brorsen explains. "It's not enough to keep sending resumes. You have to somehow stand out. By volunteering, I became a face and a personality. And the article in the paper was the clincher."

opinion on you. Your last manager if you are not working now, or the person in charge of the office in your previous job if you still are employed. You may not be on the best terms with them, but you must contact and discuss the reference they will give you. It is here you may discover the neutral recommendation. Fearing charges of slander or libel, many companies now will only confirm job title and work dates to anyone who calls for a reference. If your former employer follows those rules, so be it. Just be certain you can give a substantive reference source there as well as any official (former bosses) references.

Another way to deal with references is to work out the wording before you leave. Then there can be no fear of retribution nor will you need to worry what is being said about you.

If you think you have encountered age discrimination, the hard truth is that it's probably best to move on.

Your Age and the Job Market

Your life may begin at 40, but so too does age discrimination, at least according to the law. Many middle managers are also middle-aged, meaning they will face additional factors as they search for a new job. Discrimination against older workers is still a reality. Ironically, as the population has aged, so too has the line of demarcation. Many of us are taking better care of ourselves, so we're looking better. Out of sight, out of mind, perhaps explains some of the shift upward in age discrimination. Consequently, it's probably closer to 50 years of age that you'll begin to have to worry about age working against you. And even that may be shifting as smaller companies scarf up experienced 50-year-olds spilling out of Fortune 500 companies. Still, even at 40 you may feel the burn of discrimination in companies looking for fresh (make that cheap) blood—younger workers with fewer family obligations, more ambition, and lower wage expectations than you.

If during your search you believe you are victimized because of your age—the biggest single sign is when you start getting a series of negative reviews after years of doing well—you'll consider legal action against the firm that did it. You'll be in the same boat as you were in Chapter 2

If you've been searching more than six months, unless you are at the very senior levels of your business, you should reassess your tactics and goals.

when you considered action against your dismissal. You'll face long odds, a lot of time and the good chance of a rap on your reputation. The hard truth is that it's probably best to move on.

What You'll Feel While You Search

If you are older when you lose your job, you will probably share many of the feelings of younger workers. Money is money, status is status. Jobs are jobs. But according to a study by G. Scott Budge, a psychologist and former Pace University group-counseling specialist, older executives go through three stages.

The first is confusion, not the depression younger workers may feel. You try to deny the situation. You take vacations, don't tell family and friends what has happened, and begin your job search with an exaggerated confidence that you can find something quickly.

The second step is little better than the first. Now confusion is replaced by dismay that your life is out of control. Self-confidence erodes. You create a new routine of dressing and leaving the house. But the job hunt is neglected.

From there, the challenge is identity. The office is gone, the big salary and the perks have disappeared. The prospect of a lesser job creeps into your thinking. You blame yourself for all that has happened. Family and friends feel the strain.

In the final step you adapt, accepting that you're in a contingency situation that you can manage and that is not indefinite. You get on with your job search and if you need to, join a support group to help you through this time.

Pushing the Process

How long will your search take? There are no numbers that apply to everyone. Too many factors from what you did and where you did it to the size of your network and the zeal and skill you bring to the job hunt can play havoc with the averages.

But for middle-level managers with no exceptions

such as age (over 50 these days, as we noted), don't panic if six months or more pass before you're back on stage performing your job. If you've been searching longer than that, unless you are at the very senior levels of your business, you should reassess your tactics and goals.

A change of tactics

- **You're talking to the wrong people.** Go back to your network, get new names from other companies.

- **You're being perceived incorrectly.** Rethink your resume. You may be punching up the wrong set of a credentials for the job market of the moment.

- **You're turning people off.** Go back to the videotape and your mentors. Practice interviewing, answering questions. Maybe you're sounding tentative and unsure in interviews or cocky and headstrong.

- **You're getting killed by a bad reference.** Is someone damning you with faint praise? Have a friend or a colleague call your references on the guise of being interested in you for a job. See what's being said about you. Confront anyone putting your candidacy in the trash and find out why.

Strategy

Maybe your job hunt has hit a wall because you are not acknowledging strategic changes that have reduced your chances of getting a job. You're looking for aerospace engineering positions in Southern California at a time when the industry is hemorrhaging engineers because of defense cutbacks.

To get offers you may have to reshape your career goals and take your engineering skills to smaller high tech firms that make, say, computers or telecommunications equipment and can use your knowledge of metals technology to make their hardware.

You may have to relocate. Much of the job growth in

If you're former military, you can expect that everything from your vocabulary to your notion of effective management will be questioned.

the United States in the rest of the 1990s will take place where the sun shines best, the South and the West. You may have to go out on your own, starting a consulting business that brings in income and keeps you in contact with job prospects. You may take temporary assignments through an employment agency for temps such as Manpower Inc. Think of the one- or two-week job as a tryout—that's what your boss there will be thinking in many instances.

Don't quit looking. You won't get a job waiting for serendipity to take charge of the proceedings. There *is* a job out there for you. Despite what you feel, you are not going to be unemployed forever.

"Should you hire me, I will bring to the job 10 years' experience in the field, international accounting skills, contacts in government circles, plus a unique quality – the eerie aura you see that scares people and helps me cut through red tape."

Reprinted by permission: Tribune Media Services

From Defense to Private Sector

Making a career change, as you undoubtedly realize by now, can be a wrenching experience. But it is no more so than for those mustering out of the military or departing defense-industry jobs. You're not just looking for a job, but learning to look at your job in a different way. Everything from the vocabulary you use to your notion of effective management are put in question. You're in for culture shock and, sadly, a good deal of discrimination from a civilian workforce with fresh memories of $600 toilet seats and other extremes of military spending in the 1980s.

Fortunately, your plight has not gone unrecognized. The Pentagon has created the *Transition Assistance Program (TAP)*, which offers job and career advice to military personnel, and *Operation Transition*, which now offers advice to civilians and military personnel losing their jobs because of base closures. Much of the advice offered in these two programs will be familiar to any job seeker—how to write a resume, for instance, or go on an interview. (For more information, contact the closest transition office.)

But to win over skeptical civilian managers, you'll need more than that. One good source of advice aimed specifically at defense and military career changers is *Breakthrough: The Career Transition System for Defense Professionals.* published by The National Center for Career Change (510–837–6233), a job counseling company in Walnut Creek, Cal.

The author of *Breakthrough,* V. William Souveroff, says most defense professionals are better prepared for the civilian world than they realize. "They are already highly qualified, they just don't know which skills they have that are useful. After all, they tend to have been with one company (or in the military) for most of their careers. They've never been through the experience of looking for a job."

Here are some of Souveroff's recommendations:

Know where the customer fits in.

You are in transition with a capital T, with one foot in each arena—defense and civilian. To make a successful move you have to understand what makes the world go around in each place. A defense professional's world is dominated by technology. You make the customer adapt to the product. The private sector is driven by marketing and service—the product is adapted to the customer. You'll be selling your skills to people with that mind-set.

Homework was never more important.

Each company has its own mission, one that can be much different from even another similar company's mission. A company hires people who can help solve its specific problems, and if you don't know what they are, you won't be part of the solution. You'll learn that with rigorous research on each and every company you're interested in. You'll use your homework, too, to help you craft a resume tailored to a specific opening—the most effective way to get an interview.

Speak in whole words, not in those infamous and incomprehensible military acronyms (or IMAs).

Modify your message.

Lose the military jargon. You're heading into a demilitarized zone when you go hunting for work in the civilian world. Speak in whole words, not in those infamous and incomprehensible military acronyms (or IMAs). Skip the titles, too. You aren't going to be a GS-15 in the civilian world, or a major or a particular defense systems engineer. Titles, you'll learn, are shedding their meaning in the civilian world of project teams and self-directed work.

Use a functional resume that showcases your skills, not, as author P. J. Budahn says, one that justifies you holding your last military job. Says Budahn in *Drawdown Survival Guide* (Naval Institute Press): "If you want a good job, you must convince a civilian supervisor that you have the necessary skills. The odds are that you won't be able to do that if you're unconsciously applying for the last job you held in uniform."

Acknowledge the past.

You'll have to prove you aren't the kind of person who could be part of the process that produced one of those $600 toilet seats. One way: Tell potential employers that defense contractors have changed the way they bid on projects, that it's much more competitive now and more like the civilian world where cost is a critical issue.

Translate your skills.

Linda Friedman, a career counselor in Boca Raton, Fla., says it's critical not to underestimate military skills just because they are being criticized by civilians. Your experience as an officer means you can motivate a group to complete a task on time.

As James Challenger, the outplacement expert, notes, "Additionally, [members of] the military learn to make sound decisions, prioritize tasks, accept responsibility and apply clear logic to the problems at hand."

Challenger says one way to mellow a military bearing is by taking Toastmaster, Dale Carnegie or other courses that teach you civilian communication skills. Or, you can select a company with a reputation for having a military-style corporate culture where you will not seem so militaristic. Two of Challenger's recommendations are General Electric and DuPont.

Your Resume: Your Record at a Glance

Pity the poor resumes (and there are a lot of them out there), they get no respect from the people who count, the people who do the hiring. With all the hope and confidence you'll be placing in yours, you should hear how resumes get ripped apart, hooted over, or worse: ignored. Piles of them everywhere in the manager's office. . . and from just one ad in the paper. Heads shake in disbelief. Each week stacks go straight to the trash. Groans can be heard when the resumes inadvertently get in with "serious" mail. In fact, you may be one of the people who has scoffed at resumes that have landed on your desk.

"The number one problem with resumes is that they are poorly prepared, poorly reproduced," says Robert Nowaczyk, former vice president of human resources at the Vanguard Group in Valley Forge, Pa. "You tend to rank those people as poor planners. Number two—they make things so creative to get noticed and they end up making them distracting. You have to wonder if there is any substance there."

And now you've got to work on yours. You might not have even *looked* at your current one—if you can locate it—since you started your last job. Maybe that resume was the one you wrote right after you left college.

There's a widely held misconception about resumes that should be laid to rest as quickly as possible. A resume is not what you use to get a job. It's what you use to get an interview. Or, more precisely, it's one of the things you use, and it may not even be the most important thing.

Still, like belly buttons, you have to have one.

Why? you say, especially if you know that perhaps 80% of all jobs are gained through networking. Why not skip this chapter and go directly to that one? You're not the first person to feel that way. You can find professional career advisors who would tell you that you don't need a resume to get a job. Some health-care jobs, even those ranking as high as nurses and other professionals, are filled with a personal interview and a check of references and credentials. Maybe you hired people without them. But as quickly as you hear that resumes are unnecessary, you'll be told that everyone else has them, so you'd better, too, just to stay even with the competition.

Bottom line: A resume should prompt contact from an interviewer.

What Resumes Do

As if that were the end of it, after you have decided you have to have one, you won't find agreement on what it should look like. One page? Two? As many as it takes in case you snag an interested manager who would like to know more but has only a bare-bones one-page resume from which to judge you?

"Give me a call, I'll fill in the blanks!" you fliply respond.

That is the first thing upon which everyone agrees: A resume should prompt contact from an interviewer. "It's got to create enough interest to make it worth the call," says James Mueller, director, staffing and placement at Marriott International Inc. The answer to length and style is that you must tailor your resume to the job you are seeking and to your own experience and personality. If that means a long one, take your chances (but we'll tell you what to trim if you need to). For Mueller, and probably the majority of people you will contact, anything more than a couple of pages is irritating. "If I see four pages," Mueller opines, "I wonder if the person can be concise in their work."

Durward Wildman, a former personnel director for Hinsdale Hospital in Hinsdale, Ill., expected to see custom-tailored resumes, but not simply fashioned to reflect an applicant's unique experience.

Schwadron, Cartoonists & Writers Syndicate

"I didn't expect a resume to be a chronological history of the person. I wanted it to represent the activities that were useful to me," he explains.

For other situations, however, this "customizing" may mean listing your skills rather than a chronology of your employers. If you're "shotgunning" your resume to scores of companies in a direct mail campaign, you'll make it less focused, more general, so as to keep it in the running with other job seekers. Send your resume to a recruiter and you'll probably be asked for several rewrites as it is reshaped to fit an opportunity. Respond to an ad and you'll make it fit the job description like a custom suit. The important thing, and this may be a near-art, is to create an accurate—and compelling— portrait of yourself as the solution to a problem. But without gimmicks, cuteness or excess verbiage.

Despite all the abuse it takes, a resume can accomplish four goals of value to you in your job search.

Assess yourself.

As you write it you are forced to make an inventory of your achievements. Anyone in the throes of self-questioning or self-discovery can appreciate a vehicle to better understanding. Concisely describing just what you did at the Pointed Needle Works can help you clarify your strengths, the skills you honed there and, if you had problems, help you to understand their origins. The more you understand yourself, the more capably you will explain your attributes to others.

Get the word out.

It's an extended calling card, useful, of course, for gaining an interview but also useful as you network (see Chapter 9), providing your contacts with the necessary background to help spot opportunities for you.

Start the discussion.

A resume is an agenda for an interview. You won't have to spend time explaining the first twelve years of your professional life if it's right there for the interviewer to read. At the same time, many interviewers, having abandoned canned questions, will use the facts presented on your resume to probe your personality, your goals and your past achievements (see Chapter 11). Be prepared before you interview to expand on any point you have noted.

If not now, then later.

Finally, a resume is a memory jogger. Many firms keep files of the most impressive candidates. You may even wait a moment during a follow-up call while an interviewer or a secretary fetches your file to pull your resume. That takes the heat off both parties: You don't have to plead your case with a recitation of your past jobs, and the manager doesn't have to cover for ignorance and wonder if you're the hot prospect from Pittsburgh or the also-ran from Albuquerque.

Standing Out From the Rest

It takes a heap of mailing to make a resume hit home. According to one study, a company hires one person for roughly every 1,400 resumes that cross the mailroom floor. That's a staggering number, especially because you know you haven't sent that many resumes, or for that matter, any

A professionally typeset resume looks great, but it denies you the flexibility to edit your resume as you need to.

other letters, in your life.

But plenty have. Search firms will shotgun a client's resume to hundreds of corporations. Clients will shotgun their own resumes to as many company contacts as they can find, blindly trying to hit a job target. Students nearing graduation will pour gobs of letters into the pipeline.

With so much paperwork out there, your resume is going to get all the attention there is available under the conditions. You could hold your breath longer—30 to 60 seconds would be considered on the high end of the scrutiny scale. Under those conditions, brevity and clarity are givens for the successful resume.

You might return to your first English class for inspiration. A resume is form, style and content. We'll deal with form first, then concentrate on style and finally content.

Form

While you want to stand out from the rest, you can't do it with funny-colored paper or odd-sized resumes, at least not for the great majority of jobs. Unless you're a graphics designer, advertising layout person or work in some related profession where you will be judged on how you manipulate colors, illustrations and blocks of text, you'll lose points for anything unusual. Stick with 8½" by 11", 24 pound, 100% cotton bond paper or better if you can find it. Splurge on good quality; the effect is worth more than the cost. Ivory or white are the most acceptable colors, gray and pale blue a bit down the list mostly because black ink looks best on the first two backgrounds.

You can type your own resume if you use an electric typewriter and a film ribbon rather than fabric to ensure a uniform print. If you have a choice, use the larger pica over the smaller elite type size. True, you may have to condense some content to accommodate the fewer lines available (more on this later), but the larger type is easier to read. If you are using a word processor and printer, choose at least a letter-quality daisy wheel. A laserjet or inkjet printer, with its camera-ready type, is best. Unless they are at least 24-pin models, dot matrix printers don't yield a good enough type face for this project.

You may also have your resume professionally type-set. While attractive, this approach has a major drawback. You can't make changes such as updates or tailor the resume to a specific job opening without returning to the print shop for resetting. If you do decide to have the resume done professionally, stick with traditional and conservative type faces, generally those with serifs. (The type on this page has serifs—the bases and tops, or hooks, on letters. The printing you learned first in school is essentially sans serif, or lacking in serifs.) Helvetica and Times Roman are two good choices.

You may be asked whether you want the type "justi-fied," that is, with the type spaced so that both margins are even and straight. That is acceptable, but you should consider having it set "ragged right," which is more like typing or writing on a sheet of paper. (In recent years ragged right has become more popular in newspapers and many magazines seeking some variety from the straight columns of most periodicals.)

The issue is just how much of a professional job seeker you want to appear to be. Too slick a resume, even within the narrow definitions we are using, may make you seem like someone who does a lot of looking.

A professionally typeset and offset-printed resume may cost you $100 or more, depending on prevailing prices in your area, the paper you choose and the number of copies you order printed. The more copies you have printed at one time, the less each resume costs, so it's

By permission of Johnny Hart and Creators Syndicate, Inc.

worth the expense to have a supply on hand in case your search lasts longer than you expected.

Typing your own resume and having it printed at a quick-print shop will yield acceptable resumes for around $60 for four hundred copies, for example. But consider that your resume may be photocopied many times as it works its way through an organization. The sharper the original the better the copies will be. And as a resume is the first impression you'll be making, it might as well be the best.

No matter who does the work, be sure to have one inch margins all around. Single spaced is preferred, with some judicial spacing to separate sections and allow for easier reading.

Style

Resumes fall into two major categories and a third one that is an amalgam of the two. Each serves a particular clientele.

Chronological resumes, as the word implies, offer your experience in terms of where you worked and when you worked there, listing your last or current position at the top. *Functional* resumes abandon that format to characterize you in terms of the skills you possess. The amalgam, a *chrono-functional* resume, offers some of each.

Chronological

This is the traditional resume that lands on a thousand desks every morning. But don't knock tradition, for this is the most acceptable of the three common resume formats. That's because recruiters and employers can quickly see what you have accomplished. In less than a minute, most chronological resumes can be accurately scanned, and those candidates with potential can be moved to the active file.

Write one for yourself and you'll include the following elements: your name, address and telephone number; your career objective; a summary of what you have done already; and in some detail a description of your work history beginning with your current position and moving back. (See page 128 for an example.) A chronological resume:

- works effectively for those who have followed a single career path that they want to continue to follow.

- is a great way to show upward progress both inside a company and through a series of jobs.

- shows a prospective employer, at a glance, your rise to increasing responsibility and success.

Functional

This approach focuses attention on the skills you've mastered. Where you got them gets second billing. People use functional resumes when a chronological format might work against them.

While that includes entry-level job-seekers who don't have many credentials to wheel out, it also applies to:

- people coming back into the work force after an absence,

- those whose careers have flattened into a series of similar jobs,

- military personnel joining the civilian job force from a "lay-off" and those who are close to retirement.

In addition, people who want to downplay the bulk of the work they have performed so that they can turn their career in a new direction often use a functional resume to accomplish that.

A functional resume is also used by people who have checkered or spotty job histories, or are job hoppers. That's why functional resumes don't cut it with many people who do the hiring.

But don't rule them out. The key is to focus the content so that you have an employment objective. A scattershot functional resume simply doesn't work. Aim every word in a functional resume at a specific job target. That, of course, means you have to have a job target, so use functional resumes when you know what you're applying for—say an opening you've learned about through

Continued on page 131

Chronological Resume

Dana P. Williams
2 Park Street
Martinsburg, MO 40513
305-555-1243

EMPLOYMENT EXPERIENCE

American Amal-Gamators   1992 to date
Benson, Mo.
Manufacturer, $4 Billion Annual Sales
Director of Information Services
Responsible for all elements of company's information management, including design and installation of $12 million system, recruitment and administration of 45–person headquarters staff and additional personnel in 16 branch offices. Headed task force that recruited at three universities. Final say on all branch administrators. Led budget committee study that brought 20% savings in materials costs.

Technocratic Applications, Inc.   1987-'92
San Pedro, Cal.
National consulting and information retrieval firm
As staff member, implemented company's first work-station application. Cut travel expenses for firm by 23%, using improved system for airline reservations. Promoted to assistant director of information systems after 18 months. Interim director for four months until accepting current position at American Amal-Gamators.

Compu/Info Corp.
Sacramento, Cal.
Internship four months, 1986
Highly competitive management-track program for graduate students sponsored by Sacramento Business Guild.

EDUCATION
Detroit University, M.S., information systems, 1987
Santa Ana State, Cal., B.S., medieval literature, 1985

LANGUAGES
Fluent in Spanish; read French and German. Traveled extensively in Western Europe, Northern Africa.

Functional Resume

Dana P. Williams
2 Park Street
Martinsburg, MO 40513
305-555-1243

OBJECTIVE   A management position in information services where I can use my skills effectively as an innovator and organizer to respond to changing market conditions.

SUMMARY   More than a decade of growing information-systems design and management responsibility, most recently as the head of a 45–person headquarters staff serving 16 branch offices of a Fortune 500 corporation.

SKILLS

Systems
Designed, put out for bid and led team in selection of $12 million computer system. Oversaw installation and start up. Have managed all modifications since.

Recruiting
Managed company's information-systems recruiting at three universities. Interviewed final candidates for all branch administrators. Turnover rate under 4%, lowest in corporation.

Financial
Oversaw all budget items for division. Headed annual budget-committee meetings. Coordinated division's requirements with other divisions' data-processing needs. Cut travel expenses 23%, using improved airline-reservation system.

EMPLOYMENT EXPERIENCE

AMERICAN AMAL-GAMATORS   1992 to date
Benson, Mo.
Manufacturers of amal-style gamators. Top-five producer in world market.
Director of Information Systems. Oversee staff of 16 with annual $4 million budget.

TECHNOCRATIC APPLICATIONS, INC.   1987-'92
San Pedro, Cal.
National consulting and information-retrieval company.
Assistant director, information systems, 1989-'92
Staff, information systems, 1987-'89

EDUCATION

M.S., Detroit University, 1987; information systems
B.S., Santa Ana State, Cal., 1985; medieval literature
Fluent in Spanish; read French and German.

Chrono-Functional Resume

Dana P. Williams
2 Park Street
Martinsburg, MO 40513
305-555-1243

OBJECTIVE

A management position in information services where I can use my skills as an innovator and organizer to respond to changing market conditions.

EMPLOYMENT EXPERIENCE

AMERICAN AMAL-GAMATORS, Benson, Mo.   1992 to date
Director of Information Systems

Skills
Management
Direct staff of 45 with $8 million annual budget. Converted cost-of-living increases to merit system, saving 20% of labor costs.

Systems
Designed, put out for bid and led team in selection of $12 million computer system. Oversaw installation and start up. Have managed all modifications since.

Recruiting
Managed company's information-systems recruiting at three universities. Interviewed final candidates for all branch administrators. Turnover rate under 4%, lowest in corporation.

Financial
Assessed all budget items for division. Directed annual budget-committee meetings. Coordinated division's requirements with other divisions' data-processing needs. Cut travel expenses 23%, using improved airline-reservation system.

TECHNOCRATIC APPLICATIONS, INC., San Pedro, Cal.   1987-'92
Assistant director, information systems, 1989-'92
Staff, information systems, 1987-'89

Skills
Management
Directed staff of 12 in division distributing payroll and benefits. Cut staff 25% in 18 months.

Systems
Reduced payroll processing-time to three days from five. Department named most improved in corporation, 1988.

EDUCATION

M.S., Detroit University, 1987; information systems
B.S., Santa Ana State, Cal., 1985; medieval literature
Fluent in Spanish; read French and German.

networking, or from a newspaper ad or a posting on a company bulletin board. Don't use it for broader job hunts. Too specific a focus only plays into the process of elimination. You make yourself an early target for the reject pile because you've too narrowly defined yourself.

And unlike former times, when you might have gotten away with omitting dates of employment, you must include them now. Otherwise you will red-flag your candidacy (see the discussion under "Employment," page 134). You can lessen emphasis on dates by using years alone, without delineating your experience by the specific months you came and went and by placing this information at the end of each job description. (For an example, see page 129.)

For perspective, ask people you've worked with for their impressions of your strengths and accomplishments.

Chrono-functional

You might call this the resume of the 1990s, for it is the choice of fast-track individuals with a serious intent to climb the corporate ladder. This double-barreled approach starts with a career summary, adds a description of your functional skills and follows with a chronological history. Boom, boom, boom. If you have the professional achievement and glitter to back it up, it can be a powerful resume.

Content

Before you write more than your name and address at the top of your resume, organize your thoughts. Using work sheets, write about each of the jobs you have held, what you did, what you accomplished. You might want to ask people you've worked with (maybe even former bosses) for their impressions of your strengths and accomplishments. They might provide an interesting perspective—and remember some things you'd forgotten about. Outline your education and spend time considering what you want from your next job—and from your career.

By the time you've finished, you'll probably have written more than you can ever use. Make sure it is accurate. Check dates, names and addresses. When you're done, you will have a draft of your resume. Now it's time to assemble it, then edit it until it is concise but still reflects your style.

All this effort may seem unnecessary, especially in light of how often resumes are ill-treated. But the difference between a well-thought-out resume and a casually prepared one can make all the difference. A good resume nets a careful review and gets you an interview by a potential employer. A bad one gets chucked, or filed, which amounts to the same thing most times. For an example of how this process can yield both an unwieldy mass of words or, with some rewriting, a potent pitch, see pages 137–138.

A resume must contain certain information and may contain other facts about you. Starting from the top, which is how everyone else will look at it, here are the elements of a resume.

The top does not say "Resume."

If someone can't tell by looking that they have a resume in their hands, then you have some rewriting to do. "Fact Sheet" and "Curriculum Vitae" are out as well. They are dated, stilted and as unnecessary as "Resume." Instead, start with your name, address and home telephone number centered and single spaced. You may want to include your business number too, depending on whether you intend to receive calls in your office. You'll make a positive impression if you leave it off the resume and include it in your cover letter, admonishing prospective employers to use it with discretion.

You can leave off any "Jr.'s" or "III's" unless you are going to be easily confused with your father or grandfather. Use your first and last name and a middle initial or a first initial and your middle name if that's what you go by. You don't need to offer your full name unless you use it professionally or you need to include your maiden name for the

"I didn't bring a resume.
I don't like to dwell on the past."

From The Wall Street Journal, Permission,
Cartoon Features Syndicate

sake of references from earlier in your career. Unless there is some gender confusion—you're a Leslie or a Gale or a Carroll, for example—you need not say "Mr." or "Ms." as a precedent to your name.

Use appropriate abbreviations in your address, and place the zip code on a single line with your city and state. Your telephone number may go below that. Skip a line and it will be easier to read.

If you need it, you can save a line or two by centering

Karl Stein: Out on His Own

For Karl Stein of Dayton, Ohio, entrepreneurship has been like the slow takeoff of a rumbling jumbo jet. He's on the right track, and moving along, but he's not quite airborne. It's a place many entrepreneurs find themselves in on the road to success. The lesson: patience, and confidence in your product and plan will carry you through the development phase of creating your own business.

Stein was an engineer at NCR Corp. for ten years. When the ax fell on his career he grabbed every free piece of advice and service he could from the company, taking small business seminars it offered to outgoing employees and office space it had set aside for laid-off workers. Stein's zeal and determination are strong enough that he now gives lectures to other displaced workers on how to start their own businesses.

Stein is an inventor, having created a lint and pilling remover brush 20 years years ago that was the precursor to the woman's facial cleansing brush he's marketing now. He wisely spent nearly as much time developing a marketing plan as he did creating and devising production methods for his product. But the door that led out of his NCR career opened on a chance to make his hobby a career. "This is my job now," he says. "This is my company."

His $4.95 Facial Sensation natural-gum rubber brushes are a hit wherever he shows them, and he uses spot sales to individuals and salons to lower his expenses. He plans to extend the line to body brushes, a line of men's products including a shaving kit, and lotions and cleansers. So far, Stein has $10,000 or so invested in tools, raw materials and inventory. He has a federal trademark on the name, as well as product liability insurance and a local packager and shipper lined up when production goes up.

A major drugstore chain and a home shopping network are considering selling his brush, and he plans to market the brushes through the mail. The three-pronged plan is the key to turning his project into his long held dream of owning and operating a small company.

Says Stein, "It's moving slower than I predicted when I started, but the next time we talk I will have it."

Most people describe what they do when they really should be saying what they have accomplished.

your name at the top and placing your address to the left margin and your home phone number and, if you're using it, your business number on the right margin.

The summary

You often see the title "Job Objective" on many resumes, resting just below the name and address. In a single paragraph, candidates outline what they are seeking—and get themselves marked off the short list for countless numbers of jobs they may have wanted. That's the argument against including a specific job objective. On the other hand, you focus your resume with a brief written statement that can be easily tailored to fit the job opening while leaving the rest of the resume unchanged.

If you don't like to use "Objective," you can call this a "Summary" and make it that much easier for a manager to understand who you are and what you want. This approach can be very effective for middle managers who have had extensive experience; it doesn't work well for candidates fresh out of school who can't point to a series of work-related achievements to prove their objective is attainable.

By keeping these statements broad, you gain in another way. If you aren't considered for an immediate opening, your resume may be filed for the future. A general statement may keep you in the running for more jobs.

"Put your best foot forward," say Robert Nowaczyk, the former human relations executive. "People tend to read what is at the top of the page, so put something great up there—be it education or training or good work experience."

If you can't decide whether you want to put a summary in your resume, consider making it a part of your cover letter.

Employment

If you've chosen a chronological resume, your employment record comes next. Even if you job-hopped or worked only briefly at one or two places, you still must show the dates of your employment. Omit them and you are throwing a signal you've got something to hide. But there is a way to circumvent the issue and still be honest. You can drop the specific days and even months you came to work and left. November 1984–March 1985 becomes 1984–1985 in this format. Not inaccurate, but not terribly damning either, although you should be ready to explain your tenure to anyone interviewing you who asks. And once you use it, you must continue the style throughout your resume.

You may have worked hard for the title you have. People within your organization may understand the subtle differences between "associate" and "senior" whatever. But to the outside world you are a salesperson or a manager. Use those generic terms somewhere in your job description, especially if the title you hold is ambiguous. You can also shed some lower-ranking titles, becoming an accountant, for instance, rather than the *junior* accountant title that you hold. You are an accountant, after all.

Some professionals, those working in fields with few players or where confidentiality is critical, may want to keep the name of their current employer out of their resume. But that instance is unusual and you should name the company where you work.

Don't list part-time jobs unless you have to, if, say, you're shifting to a new career and want some proof you're doing a smart thing. Don't say when you're available unless that is an issue—you're in a summer executive training program you'll complete in two months, for instance. Save the line on your resume. An employer will assume you can come to work within a reasonable time. Don't give reasons for leaving. That only invites speculation and misunderstanding. Let the assumption be that you left happy and for a better opportunity. The exception may be if you left several jobs to continue your education and want no misunderstandings about chronology and your work record.

Don't list your salary at any job. Let that matter come up later in your job hunt, when it will be meaningful.

Your responsibilities

Here you must do your best to make each word work for you. There are ways to say you're good and then there

Resume Action Verbs	
Achieved	Led
Approved	Managed
Built	Negotiated
Completed	Organized
Conducted	Planned
Controlled	Produced
Converted	Promoted
Created	Reduced
Delivered	Simplified
Designed	Sold
Developed	Solved
Directed	Started
Doubled	Strengthened
Earned	Supervised
Edited	Terminated
Eliminated	Trained
Established	Transformed
Expanded	Translated
Founded	Trimmed
Generated	Tripled
Headed	Verified
Improved	Won
Increased	Worked
Installed	Wrote
Instituted	
Invented	
Launched	

are ways to make you sound extraordinary. Same work, same you, just a different set of words. Most people describe what they *do* when they should be saying what they *accomplished*. In fact, "accomplished" is one of the action verbs you will want to use in your resume. See the list on the previous page for others.

Reading the list can give you a sense of the tone and spirit you want your resume to convey. You want anyone reading it to know you were not just a hired hand signed on for a few years until you got bored. You did things. Things happened when you were on the job. You reduced the time it took to make a product, you planned a program from scratch or you foresaw a problem before it was obvious. In short, there was change—for the better.

While you are preparing your resume, take time to quantify those achievements. We live in a time when numbers carry weight and statistics fascinate. Compute the dollar savings you brought to your company when you reorganized the sales department. Measure the percentage of growth in production that came when you took over the management of the print shop. If one of your responsibilities was acquisition—land, machinery, vehicles— measure the dollar value of those purchases, and the quantity, and include those figures in your resume.

As you consider what you've done, organize the results around these measures.

- **You did more with the same resources.** Whether that was staff, budget or materials, if you show you upped performance without raising the cost, say it.

- **You made things simpler.** Music to any company's ears, especially when you did it with the obvious, something everyone else had overlooked. You shortened the route from one plant to another. You reorganized the warehouse so things flowed from one end to the other.

- **You attained something for the first time.** You'll be appreciated for everything from bringing overtime under control to making a customer out of a longtime holdout.

Continued on page 139

A Resume Facelift: Before

KEVIN TICHTMAN

2804 FESTOR CT.
BOWIE, MD 20716

w. 202-555-8188
h. 301-555-1958

OBJECTIVE:

Degreed professional with experience in retirement housing, client relations, marketing and administration, having excellent written and verbal communication skills, computer skills (Wordperfect, Lotus 1-2-3, MS DOS) and familiarity with property management, finance and accounting seeks to obtain a position in retirement housing as a leasing consultant or marketing manager.

EXPERIENCE:

American Corporation for Housing: 1988 to present - Public relations liaison ("Investor Correspondent") for general partner of multi-family and retirement housing developer/operator. Provide information support for owners of rental retirement and other multi-family projects with information on operations, property management activities and other due diligence through verbal and written communications. Produce disposition disclosure materials. Analyze project budget and financial data, work with property managers, research and write partnership correspondence. Meet production deadlines for distribution of tax and other vital partnership information. Exercise knowledge of limited partnership structure, real estate finance, apartment operations, government housing programs and tax laws in daily interaction with investors, brokers, attorneys and real estate professionals.

First Hyattstown Securities: 1985 to 1987 - Registered securities representative for discount stock brokerage. Administered investment product marketing and trading services, execution of security trades (domestic and foreign stocks, bonds, mutual funds and options) and providing customer services including, investment information, trading problem resolution, securities transfer, delinquent account collection and regulatory compliance.

Arundel Shareholder Services Corp. (a.k.a. Arundel Group): 1984-1985–Broker services representative for national mutual fund and investment company. Provided product information, transaction related services, and customer support for institutional brokerage accounts. Provide investment analysis, money and securities transfer, problem resolution and other services for shareholders and institutional marketing staff.

EDUCATION & PROF. LICENSES:

B.A., Univ. of Maryland (1983) - Major in government, minor in economics.
Professional licenses: NASD Series 7 & 63 (1985), Maryland Health and Life Insurance (1988).

A Resume Facelift : After

KEVIN TICHTMAN

2804 FESTOR CT.
BOWIE, MD 20716

w. 202-555-8188
h. 301-555-1958

PROFESSIONAL ACCOMPLISHMENTS

More than six years of experience in customer service, public relations and sales. Areas of expertise include:

- **Customer Service**
- **Mutual Fund Sales**
- **Municipal Bond Sales**
- **Insurance Sales**
- **Retirement Plans**
- **Verbal & Written Communication**
- **Information Services**
- **Multi-Family Real Estate Investment**
- **Accounting & Finance**
- **IBM PC (Lotus & Wordperfect)**

EMPLOYMENT HIGHLIGHTS

American Corporation for Housing

March 1988 to present

Public Relations Liaison ("Investor Correspondent")

Provided public relations, information support and customer service for retirement housing and multi-family developer/operator. Wrote partnership correspondence to investors. Analyzed operations and leasing activities of rental retirement developments. Resolved customer disputes.

The Prudential/PRUCO Securities

November 1987 to March 1988

Account Executive

Marketed financial planning services. Sold life insurance and other investment products including term, whole and variable life, mutual funds, partnerships, REITs and other investments.

First Hyattstown Securities

October 1985 to October 1987

Registered Securities Representative

Sold mutual funds, municipal bonds and other investment products. Traded domestic and foreign stocks, bonds, mutual funds and options. Provided customer services. Collected delinquent accounts.

Arundel Shareholder Services Corp. (a.k.a. Arundel Group)

February 1984 to October 1985

Broker Services Representative

Provided customer service for mutual fund investment company. Serviced retirement plan investments. Provided marketing support for brokerage accounts.

EDUCATION & PROFESSIONAL LICENSES

B.A., University of Maryland (1983); major in government, minor in economics.
Professional licenses: NASD Series 7 & 63 (1985); Maryland Health and Life Insurance (1988).

While you are tooting the horn about your accomplishments you will also be touting your skills. Don't make the mistake of saying things like this: you are strong on leadership, or you get along well with people or you command loyalty. Of course you do. So does everyone. There are more specific skills you should be promoting. Skills such as analyzing, designing, communicating, directing and supervising, planning and problem solving. You offer new approaches to ideas, you're a good listener. You have an excellent memory, you have mechanical skills. These are talents and abilities an employer seeks. If you have them, say so.

One way to help you discover these skills is to pick several experiences in your work life—jobs, situations, projects—that you really liked. What was it about those assignments that made you happy? Incorporate the reasons into your resume. In the process, you may discover more about yourself than your realized, and that could lead to new career choices.

You can also list professional affiliations, but don't add religious or political links unless they are appropriate for the job.

Don't let resume hype lead you to exaggeration. Leave out the jargon of your business unless it is an appropriate shorthand way to describe something you did. Don't make any demands in your resume and don't talk about your weaknesses.

"It helps to be a little crazy to work here, but you're overqualified."

Schwadron, Cartoonists & Writers Syndicate

139

Don't use your cover letter to solve your problem, but make it an offering to solve the reader's.

On functional and chrono-functional resumes, present your job responsibilities in the form of a listing of accomplishments. Use the action words described above to make each one as positive as possible. (See the resume examples on pages 128, 129 and 130 to compare how the same job history is presented in the three formats.)

Besides action words, you must include keywords, words that quickly identify your skills. Why? Because today many resumes are optically scanned, especially those that are filed on line or on the Internet. These scanners search for keywords, mostly nouns, that reveal specific aspects of your career. Resumes containing those words survive the winnowing process.

For example, in health care, the computer might search for *assisted living* as a keyword. That's a growing area of housing for the elderly. In human resources, the keywords might be *defined contributions*, or *401(k)*, two words that reveal you're part of the fastest growing area in retirement planning. Keywords in computing would include *servers, JAVA* and *URLs*. All are related to the Internet. Professional affiliations that lead to certification and thus measure—you're a financial planner with a *Certified Financial Analyst* designation is a good example.

For more keywords, check the classified ads in your career area, noting the kinds of key nouns—licensing, certification, affiliation—you see again and again. Recruiters and those who have recently found jobs may also know which keywords yield the best results.

Education

Just how much space you devote to your academic laurels depends on how long ago you graduated and the kind of job you are seeking. Since you've probably been working for some time, education can be written off with one or two lines that state the school, the major and the date of graduation. You'll list highest degree first, and end it with the baccalaureate. Omit high school unless it was very prestigious and you feel it might help your chances.

If you didn't graduate, give the dates you attended a college or university, but again, leave off high school or it will brand you as little more than a college dropout. People with extensive experience but no sheepskin should emphasize the academic programs they did complete—seminars, classes, short-term executive programs.

Of course, if you are seeking academic work, you will want to place much more emphasis on your scholastic achievements.

The rest of the resume

There probably shouldn't be anything else on your resume. No personal data, no hobbies, nothing about race, marital status, country of origin, sex, political affiliation or the like. Most of those are off-limits to employers anyway because of anti-discriminatory laws. This information has little real bearing on your qualifications—unless you are applying to work in a political party's headquarters, for example.

The same holds true if you have a handicap. Don't make it an issue before its time.

No photographs and no gimmicks. No cute lines or jokes.

You can add "references available upon request" if you are using a functional resume and you feel you need to further reassure anyone reading your resume that you are qualified. Otherwise, it will be assumed you have references. After all, if you don't you have a big problem. Don't list any information about your references but have their names and telephone numbers printed on a sheet of paper you can distribute at interviews.

Cover Letters

Cover letters don't fare much better than resumes, and they frequently deserve that fate. You've probably read plenty yourself. Too often they begin with a dry recitation of what is contained in the resume, followed by hollow

Continued on page 143

Cover Letter

Dana P. Williams
2 Park Street
Martinsburg, MO 40513
305-555-1243

June 6, 1997

Martin Arnold, President
Pacific Industries
77 Rutgers Ave.
Plainfield, KS 67831

Dear Mr. Arnold:

Over the past few months I've had the pleasure of meeting with your director of planning, Janet Andrews. In the course of one of our conversations, she described a position in information systems now open at Pacific Industries. When we talked further, I realized my background in systems information for the American Amal-Gamators Corp. and earlier with Technocratic Applications, Inc. may well fit your needs.

My M.S. in information systems led me first to Technocratic, where I implemented the company's first work-station application. I cut travel expenses by 23% using an improved system of airline reservations. At American Amal-Gamators I supervised a 45-person headquarters staff and additional personnel in 16 branches. I headed the task force that recruited at three universities and designed the installation of a $12 million computer system.

I believe I could make similar contributions to your company, cutting travel costs, for example, or ensuring the lowest installation cost for your new computer system.

I will call you next week to arrange for an interview. I look forward to our conversation.

Sincerely,

Dana P. Williams

Enclosure

claims of qualification and incredible enthusiasm for the work. They end with the hopeless wish the reader will contact them, something they await. One hopes no one is holding any breath.

Want to make a cover letter sing? Don't use it to solve your problem, but make it an offering to solve the reader's. Your cover letter can be an excellent place to convince a manager you actually do know something about the company, its achievements and its challenges. You mean it when you say you can offer something if you explain in your letter just what you could give.

Candidates who get interviews are people who show companies they are truly interested in the product. How?

A company that engineers quality products wants people who are excited about their products. Check out the newest shoes, or hair spray, of the company you're considering, and mention it in your letter.

Another angle: If you know a manufacturer is moving into a broader product line and you have the necessary experience, say that in your cover letter. Tell them you helped develop new products, or you have set up assembly lines or initiated marketing campaigns. The point is to plug your skills into a specific opening, not simply American Amalgamated Manufacturing. This is not the same as being too specific in your resume. Here you're saying that you know exactly what they want. How do you know? You will have uncovered that information when you've done your research on companies that interest you, as outlined in Chapter 8.

Hit a manager with an opening paragraph that solves a company problem and you're halfway to an interview. Take the next paragraph to make your pitch. Nothing needs to be very long; you have a resume for the details. In a final paragraph say you will phone for an interview. Don't wait for someone to call you. Besides, with this tactic you can then honestly say when you call that the person is expecting you—you did warn them.

There in three paragraphs you have made your point and announced your intentions. (For an example of a cover letter, see page 142.)

Since the cover letter is a sort of wrapping—the first thing that gets read, in most instances, when you apply for work—consider spending a little more on its production than you do on the resume. Rather than offset printed or inexpensive embossed (raised) lettering, get engraved stationery on heavy, 24 pound bond. Not every commercial printer does engraved stationery, but most stationery and card shops and office supply stores can fill your order, although delivery can take several weeks. A set of 250 letter-sized sheets and matching envelopes in a high-quality bond will cost you more than $200 in most instances. But you will have it for follow-up and reminder letters and your own personal business. (Although cover letters will probably always be a single page, consider getting a small supply of blank sheets in case you ever need a second page.) Once the original die is cut, reordering prices drop significantly from the cost of your first purchase.

Campaign Letters

Just as functional and chronological resumes can be merged, you can also combine a cover letter and a resume into what has been variously called a personal salesletter or a campaign letter. They are better suited for executive level jobs than beginning or lower-level management jobs or where a resume has been specifically requested. They are also more effective when you are seeking information about a company or where you are not angling for a current opening but want to make contact nonetheless. You can use them when you know a job opening is upcoming—you're privy to a friend's successful job search, for instance, and want to apply for the soon-to-be-vacated position.

Address the letter to an individual, not a department. As you would with the "employment" section of your resume, describe some of your best achievements. Use the action verbs we noted earlier. Make your pitch. The success you created at one job is transferable to the next. While you're tooting your horn, however, leave out the names of current or past employers and never mention salary. You are fishing here for whatever the job sea will yield.

Continued on page 146

Campaign Letter

Dana P. Williams
2 Park Street
Martinsburg, MO 40513
305-555-1243

June 6, 1997

David Shipley
Straight Edge Industries
Hoover, UT 84601

Dear Mr. Shipley:

As director of information systems, I supervise a staff of 45 with an annual budget of $8 million. I've converted an uninspiring across-the-board bonus plan into a spirited merit system that has cut 20% off the department's annual labor costs. I did it and managed to reduce turnover to 4% in the process. That's the lowest in the division.

I can do the same for you. That's why I'm writing. I'm seeking a new opportunity, and my research has led me to your company. With an annual growth rate of 22%, Straight Edge is the leader in a competitive market. I like that. I'm a native of the Southwest (Arizona) who longs to return. And I'm eager to see your patented "Sidebar Modulator" in action. I know it generated a lot of excitement here when we read about it in *Information Systems Journal.*

I will call your office next week to arrange an interview. I look forward to meeting with you.

Sincerely,

Dana P. Williams

With the second paragraph you announce your intentions. You are introducing yourself. You'd like to explore any opportunities available within the firm for someone with your talents and experience.

With a third paragraph you return to your achievements, while a fourth describes your education. You can close with an invitation to meet. Here you will be less forceful than with a cover letter. This is only a fishing expedition. Be sure to type "personal and confidential" on the envelope. Sometimes that keeps the letter from being shunted by a secretary to the personnel department. (An example of campaign letter is on page 145.)

Why bother with this? Variety for one thing. You escape the pack of job seekers who just put resumes in the mail. Often a personal letter with more meat in it than a cover letter will draw the attention of managers bleary-eyed from the former. It's another opportunity to showcase your communication skills so consider using it in addition to the resumes and cover letters, networking and interviews that comprise your job hunt.

Take Time for Perfection

Proofread everything you send out. If you have it, use the spell-check feature on your word-processing software. Have someone else proofread it, too, because it is too easy to overlook mistakes and a spell-checker can't catch everything; it may not catch repeated words and it won't tell you when your turn of phrase is unclear. Double check names and addresses as well. Your resume is the first piece of your work a potential employer sees. If you couldn't even get that right, what are your prospects as an employee?

"Your resume should be your very best foot forward," says former personnel director Durward Wildman. "It ought to be a perfect document."

Make Your Homework Count

Job hunting is a two-way street. You know you'll be checked out by a company when you apply for work, but you should also be checking out companies, and doing much of it before you mail a single resume or call for an interview. After all, there's a lot at stake here beyond getting a paycheck again. You've got a career to manage at a time when you're asking a lot of questions of yourself and where you fit into the work picture. The last thing you want is another round of job hunting in a couple of years. Besides, you're only going to make a first impression once. Because companies have a nasty habit of pigeonholing candidates rather quickly, you could wind up judged and found wanting before you've had a chance to tailor your resume and cover letter and target your application.

Researching is like detective work. You play sleuth, running down leads, circling names in the paper, reading company profiles and annual reports. The case you're on is you.

The clues are everywhere. You must be certain you overlook none of them during your investigation. The net you are casting in search of a job must reach everywhere, so besides your resume and your network, you must spend time reading and listening with a trained eye and ear for opportunity.

Chances are you know quite a lot about a lot of firms already from earlier job hunts, contacts you've had with

You're likely to find out more than you ever imagined—inside scoops, opportunities, contacts.

your counterparts, and the stories friends, colleagues and relatives have told you about a given company. But you probably weren't looking for work then and now you are. So your homework must be of a higher caliber, and this chapter will help you make it such.

There Is a Lot to Learn

Your search for a place to work will mean finding companies that look promising and have openings you might like in places you'd like to live. But there's more than mere opportunity to be ferreted from the facts. You'd be joining an ongoing enterprise with a history, goals and a corporate culture, stepping into a complex situation with myriad variables, any one of which can spoil your chances for success. How has the company survived competition? Is the company bulging with employees and ripe for payroll cuts? What are its strengths and weaknesses? What has it failed at in the past? What was its biggest success? Who succeeds there? Where would you fit in?

Your research pays with more than names. As important as finding opportunity is avoiding disasters. While searching for names you may discover the company is facing serious legal battles over a trademark or the division is about to be spun off to management, a move that will surely lead to a shake-up. You may also discover an old nemesis lurking in the upper echelons.

You may discover an old mentor or see the real opportunity for you lies not in marketing but in a joint venture the firm has with an old customer of yours. You may see an untapped lead you can share with the firm when you interview. In looking thoroughly at one firm (which you may realize you don't like at all) you may discover another that interests you more. You go to Portland, Ore., for an interview with Catalina Swimwear and end up liking Freightliner, the truck maker, better.

Armed with such a thorough background on a company, you may discover jobs that aren't yet available but will be. Or, in the course of your research you may pick up signs of a change in direction that mean the company will be looking for you in a little while. It's time to bolster the German operation, you discover the CEO saying in a recent speech you're reading about in *Forbes*. For you the news is especially welcome. You speak the language. You know the business. You did a two-year stint in Stuttgart in the early '80s. But you don't hit the CEO up for a job, you check one of the business profile books we've listed, *The Corporate Yellowbook,* for instance, to find the head of international development. To her you send the letter which reviews some of what you know and you follow up with a phone call. The interview is on Thursday!

"Retirement plan? I wouldn't worry about that. You'd be out of your mind to work here that long."

From The Wall Street Journal, Permission, Cartoon Features Syndicate

In a variation on the preceding theme, this time you suggest your role. In Stuttgart the company will need new supply sources. You know them. Rather quickly, the discussion settles on responsibilities, titles and compensation.

If you like what you see the search moves on to discovering who is doing the hiring where you want to work. You can't get successful interviews if you don't have names and titles, biographies and histories to guide you to the right person. Too many times job seekers underestimate the power of a good background check. Too often they end up in the wrong division, talking to the wrong person about the wrong job, while two corridors away, the right one goes begging.

You get past a lot of corporate chaff and into real job territory. You've pinpointed where you want to go. You know how to ask directions to get there. You know marketing is your business but you understand the software division is already a write-off the company is looking to unload. You'd look nice there as window dressing for the sale, but you can talk your way into the up and coming export division where things are hot.

Turning yourself into a walking corporate

You may feel it, you may smell it—the mood and attitude, the practices and customs that reside a level below policy.

encyclopedia isn't just useful as a preamble to a job search. You bolster your position in an interview (as well as your cover letter) when you use what you have learned to show you are someone with enough ambition and interest to have checked out the company. Unless you have sat on the other side of the table, you can't appreciate what a turnoff an ignorant interviewee can be—wasting time, insulting the situation with what amounts at best to indifference if not laziness.

There are many sources of information on jobs, companies and people we will detail at the end of this chapter. But before you start your search, let's take a look at corporate culture. Learning if a place is right for you is as important as discovering a company with a job opening.

Finding the Right Corporate Culture for You

Tom Peters, the management guru, calls it the way a place smells. You might say corporate culture is the way a place feels. When it feels wrong—the mood and attitude, the practices and customs that reside a level below policy—it's like an allergy. The moment you arrive, your chest tightens, your head gets stuffy.

Of course, when you're compatible with your company's culture, it's like soothing background music. You just do a better job. You're understood, your work is effective. Your circle of friends probably includes plenty of people you met at the office.

Having a nice day at the office isn't the only reason to pay attention to corporate culture. Much more is at stake. Says Ralph Kilmann, director of the Program in Corporate Culture at the University of Pittsburgh, "Employee involvement is *the* notion of the 1990s. But in many organizations, employees are only giving 20% of what they could."

Kilmann blames that on lousy corporate cultures.

"You can buy technology but you can't buy a corporate culture that works."

"Our only saving grace," he adds, "is that everyone has been slow to change."

Slow change or not, you've got to know as much as you can about a company's culture before you take a job there. Your critique begins early in the process, during research and networking when you're asking a lot of questions about a firm. If you consider what you're seeking, much of it does relate to culture. "What's it like to work here?" must have been one of your first questions. You want to know the attitude, the mood of the office.

- Do they treat people fairly?

- What's the boss's style?

- How closely will you be supervised?

- Will you have a free hand to ask questions, to propose new solutions to problems?

- Will you be rewarded for good work?

- Will you succeed?

All along, the bottom-line question is: Is this a job to take, or to pass up?

There's a direct link between these questions and corporate culture. So, as you compile names and company profiles, keep notes on the culture you're discovering. What will you find?

Determining the Culture

No matter the culture that suits you, there are some signs, some *hallmarks*, of different environments. As you proceed with your job search, continue your sleuthing into the corporate culture, right through interviewing and up to the point you consider accepting an offer.

Are you greeted properly?

How a company treats an outsider says a lot about how it treats an insider. Were you welcomed and given a seat? Offered refreshments? Kept company? Or were

Were you asked to be patient or left sitting there with no explanation? Most times companies show their manners in little ways.

you herded into what was little more than a holding pen for applicants?

Are you kept waiting?

Were you asked to be patient or left sitting there with no explanation? It's possible you arrived twenty minutes after a major crisis unfolded, but most times companies show their manners in these little ways. The ramifications can grow to include how long it might take to process your insurance claim, how soon your botched vacation credit might be fixed or how much time might pass before getting plane reservations for your next business trip.

Observe other employees.

As you walk the halls toward your appointment take note of how people react to you. A few friendly faces says the company encourages employees to work as a team. If you're with the boss, how is she or he being greeted? First names? Casually? Or is it a tense exchange? Averted eyes and nervousness? That could tell you something is wrong—the boss is a tyrant, or he or she is on the way out.

What are people wearing?

Shirts and ties, women in business suits or more formal dresses says this is a company that promotes a uniform image and wants conformity. No ties, but slacks and sweaters means the culture allows more individual expression. What are you accustomed to? What do you like? A tie in itself is most times no big deal, unless the air conditioning goes. But formal dress may reveal more formal lines of communication, of power, of tasks. Lines you'll have to follow in order to succeed.

Does everybody have the same working condition?

You can judge whether that's the case when you interview with a company and get the five-cent tour. See the maintenance staff working out of the broom closet while everyone in advertising has a three-window office, and you're not witnessing the results of a company that cares equally about all of its employees.

That inequality can translate into how your career proceeds. For example, a company bragging about its research and development skills is probably putting its money behind those efforts—and promoting those people who excel there. What's that leave for someone in finance or accounting?

A host of other factors can be clues.

Is the place clean? Are desks cluttered or neat? Is there a cafeteria? Is the food good? Parking? What's the company newsletter like? Is it cordial, or stupid sounding and ineffective (suggesting perhaps that the company doesn't have a serious interest in communicating with its employees).

Employee awards and company achievement plaques are prominently displayed. The softball team scores are on the bulletin board. The retirement dinner photos are framed and hung on the wall in the cafeteria. Tickets to the theater are up for grabs, as are the company's box seats at the ballpark. The company provides stress or blood-pressure testing clinics. There is a nurse on duty. A medicine cabinet with free aspirin and Band-Aids is provided.

Read the annual report.

You probably did this long before, as part of your research and for background in your interview. But look at it for what it says about the way the company does business. Its tone, loose or formal, is revealing. So, too, if the report talks about programs such as child care for its employees or company-wide plans to boost quality. Temper your consideration, however, with the knowledge that most annual reports are meant to be slick public relations tools as well as reports on a company's activities.

Know the company's financial health.

You can learn much from the annual report, the rest from your library research. A company facing the brink

What's the company bragging about? What is it proud of? What are the little perks?

Sure, you say you can adapt yourself to any situation, but try to imagine yourself working there daily for the next 10 years.

offers a culture much different from one flush with cash. The former may reward you for using a cheap hotel when you travel, the latter may worry you're undercutting the company's first-class image. During the interview process if you are offered reimbursement for travel, hotel and food, err toward the frugal until you're surer of the company's expectations.

Talk to people who know the company.

Don't overlook people who work there now or alumnae with recent ties to the company. They can offer fresh insights of the highest level of accuracy—firsthand accounts—of what's going on in a company. They may have axes to grind or a limited viewpoint, but they were there, and for an extended period of time. (They can also supply the names of those who really rule, and those are the people you want to meet.)

Dozens and dozens of these little signs tell the story of the company's culture, how it wants things to be on the job. As insignificant as they may be individually, collectively they speak volumes. Look for them. And decide if you like what you see and hear. Sure, you say you can adapt yourself to any situation, but try to imagine yourself working there day in and day out for the next 10 years. If that prospect disturbs you, think twice about continuing with your interest in that company.

How It Works at One Company

Plenty of companies are known as much by their culture as by their products: IBM's white shirts and gray suits (declining in practice, but still strong), Microsoft's open-collared casualness but dedication to long hours, 3M's rewards for ideas from its employees, Hallmark Cards, as familial and close as the ads on television.

Indeed Hallmark serves as an example of the key role a culture can play through your job search and beyond.

For Hallmark, with one of the largest creative staffs in the world, your ability to do the job is only the baseline.

Each year, from the more than 3,000 portfolios it receives, the company finds hundreds of artists with sufficient talent. From that pile, some 100–150 are invited in for interviews, each of them qualified for the job. The culling process seeks something else, not surprising if you consider the aura that surrounds Hallmark. A company that sells goodness, whose motto is famous ("When you care enough..."), can't afford to be a rotten place to work; it would show up in the product. What Hallmark values is compatibility. Will you fit into what is a strongly defined culture that by virtue of its product has to be benign, yet efficient and profitable?

"We're looking for highly imaginative and creative team players," says Jani Mohr, a director of creative staffing and development. "Lively, warm and curious people who are out-of-the-box thinkers."

"We want well-traveled people with a world view who are fascinated by social trends and directions. People who enjoy the art of storytelling, who are keen observers of human interactions and relationships."

From the 3,000 inquiries, a scant 75 will be offered jobs and 85% will accept, a high ratio. So carefully are they screened that fewer than half a dozen of those who accept will leave Hallmark each year.

On the technical side, the theme is the same.

"We want people who can work in a team, who can lead and manage a team," says Tim Moran, corporate staffing manager. "People who fit in here are competent in their field but are comfortable in a setting where people genuinely care about each other."

Cathy© 1996 Cathy Guisewite. Reprinted with permission of UNIVERSAL PRESS SYNDICATE. All rights reserved.

On-line or the old-fashioned way, your research will pay.

If you read that with anticipation, and some curiosity about life in Kansas City, you were probably responding to the culture of Hallmark Cards, not the corporate bottom line (which is healthy) or the ability to advance (it promotes from within). You see how important corporate culture is? By the same token, if you dismissed this description, then you are perhaps more goal- and performance-oriented. Don't fret. Plenty of corporate cultures very unlike Hallmark will appeal to you—companies that value individual enterprise, the closed deal, intra-corporate competition. Besides, you probably wouldn't have made it through Hallmark's screening anyway.

You may sense the value of culture in another way. Reading those lines about Hallmark's people orientation, you may have thought that would be the perfect attitude for you to have were you to interview with Jani Mohr or Tim Moran. Score one for you.

Getting Started

Research in the 1990s is an exciting, sometimes challenging, activity. Where once you hunted through newspaper clippings and annual reports, now you can scroll menus on electronic screens. Databases can call up literally hundreds of stories, reports and analyses on thousands of companies. You can sort for companies in your field, or verify names and addresses so your search is almost 100% accurate. There's no better reason to be computer trained than to help you find the right next job.

That is not to say you can't do research the old-fashioned way. Libraries are still filled with books and periodicals in their original form. But you can't ignore the electronic search if you hope to have all the information you need to find the right job for you.

First the more familiar sources.

Read Trade Journals and Newsletters

If you haven't started already, you should be reading your industry's trade journals. Nobody moves in your business, literally, without some scribe making note of it. However seriously you took them in the past, now these trade journals and newsletters are a key source for jobs and contacts. They provide up-to-the-minute news on change in your field. And it is change upon which your search is borne. Movement means openings, expansion means opportunity, and names mean network to you.

Who got promoted? Do you know her? Him? Call with congratulations or drop a note. Let things lead to lunch, to news of what's happening in the company. To an invitation for an interview with the division head.

New products? They'll need marketing. Make a suggestion on contacts in Europe. Or a second line tailored to a related market segment. Follow it up with lunch and the interview with the division head. On and on go your networks. All from an announcement in a trade journal.

"There's always a place in our organization for a fine, compassionate human being—but he must have the killer instinct, too."

From The Wall Street Journal, Permission, Cartoon Features Syndicate

Newsletters may be more expensive than trade journals, so you'll have to weigh the cost versus the benefits to you. Among their advantages, newsletters often condense pertinent material from many sources and save you time and the expense of several subscriptions.

Your library may receive many of these publications. Check there if you don't want subscriptions.

Use the Want Ads to Advantage

Don't overlook the want ads. They complement your other sources, providing you with listings of companies *currently* looking for people. You can match what you learn about companies from all of your other research with those companies advertising they are in the market to hire. Even if you don't see the classifieds as

The classifieds may give you a good idea of who's hiring, even if you don't want the jobs that are listed.

a source of jobs—and most often they are not—once in a while they pay off. Marla S. Lewis, who until recently surveyed readers of *Traveler* magazine at the National Geographic Society in Washington, D.C., found that position advertised in *The Washington Post.* Fresh out of an MBA program, she responded to a blind ad from a "prestigious nonprofit publisher." A week later she was interviewing for the job. Afterward, she discovered that everyone in her department had been hired off similar blind ads, a procedure the Society finds successful because of the large number of skilled workers in the Capital area.

A top ad source for job leads is the *National Employment Weekly* published by *The Wall Street Journal.* Hang on to your pile of want ads. They are an important source over time of information on job titles, recurring openings, and contact names. A company that looked for a programmer in the spring will likely be doing it in the fall when you can once more make contact. Just as importantly, a company that searched six months ago for an accounting vice president may still be looking to fill that very same position.

Many newspapers publish special business sections, often on Monday, that may also contain job ads and news about expanding local business. Also check for single-topic inserts in newspapers that might be in your area. Scout those for names, more opportunities and basic information on companies you may be targeting for a new job. Look for stories about new ventures, performance of an existing division, new products; all of this is information you can use to spot specific jobs and in your interview show you know what you want and what a given company has to offer.

The explosive growth of the Internet and on-line services has opened broad new opportunities for job hunting. A plethora of electronic want ads sites on the Internet has brought an avalanche of postings.

You can surf through them, responding to those you're interested in. You can add your resume to the thousands already on line. Just how lucky you'll be at finding a job is still unknown, however. The services are too new to have reliable track records, though at least you'll get a feel for what jobs are open and what skills and qualifications are in demand.

The real strength of electronic job hunting may lie instead in its usefulness as a research tool. You can track down company names and addresses on America On Line, for example, or learn about company performance on Prodigy. Many magazines and newspapers maintain on-line or Internet sites you can tap for more information. BusinessWeek, for example, is available to AOL subscribers. You can search back issues using key words.

On Prodigy you can tap Hoover's business profiles, invaluable capsule histories of hundreds of major publicly traded companies and Strategic Investor, another source of information on individual companies.

Don't overlook the on-line "bulletin boards" where you can exchange information and job leads with others who are on-line. That's an excellent way to network.

As you can surmise, AOL appears to dominate what would be the job and career on-line business. Indeed, rapidly-growing AOL is at this writing the overwhelming choice for job hunters because of its own career advice section, its ease of Internet access and the many sources of information on business.

Tap Your Broker's Data Banks

If you're an investor in the market, you may already know about a number of research publications that study America's corporations and report on them. Such organizations include *Value Line* and *Standard & Poor's* or *Moody's Investors Service*. Brokerages produce reams of research on the companies they cover that outline corporate strategies and performance.

Do Some Primary Research

Some hands-on experience is useful. If you were scouting Motorola, for example, you would check out

continued on page 162

Reference Tools for Your Search

The following are a number of resources you should refer to when scouting out a company. Many are available at your local library. All include addresses and telephone numbers. You can use these directories to find officers' and managers' names and their exact titles.

In addition, you can find myriad directories categorized by particular industries, such as aerospace, high tech and retailing. However, because of their more specialized and thus limited use, you may have to travel to more specialized libraries such as those at business schools to find these volumes.

- *America's Corporate Families* (Dun & Bradstreet Information Services, Murray Hill, N.J.). This directory covers 11,000 corporations and their 73,000 subsidiaries, with information on number of employees, lines of business, names of officers and directors.

- *The Corporate Yellowbook* (Leadership Directories, Inc., New York). This is a fast-read source of names and direct-dial numbers for key officers in the top 1,000 corporations in the U.S. Of added value are the names and affiliations of outside board members. The directory is indexed four ways—by people, by state, by industry and by subsidiaries and divisions.

- *Directory of Corporate Affiliations* (National Register Publishing Co., Inc. New Providence, N.J.). The subtitle says a lot: "Who Owns Whom." Altogether three volumes listing information on public, private and international companies, including company divisions or subsidiaries and parent companies. Emphasis on numbers over names. The directory lists assets, liabilities, net worth and approximate sales as well as chief officers of divisions and above. It also includes information on mergers, acquisitions or name changes affecting the companies.

- *Encyclopedia of Associations* (Gale Research Co., Detroit, Mich.). Read this and you'll conclude there is an association for every conceivable interest group. (See the Flying Funeral Directors and the Alliance of Transylvanian Saxons for proof.) It's valuable for names of executive directors, addresses and as a way to separate lead associations with hundreds or thousands of members from ancillary ones with perhaps a handful of members. With that you can plan your job search to target either, depending on your interests.

- *Encyclopedia of Business Information Sources* (Gale Research, Detroit, Mich.). If abrasives are your business or interest, you can use this to find companies in the business. The encyclopedia offers 24,000 information sources for 1,100 specific subjects. Among the sources are bibliographies, abstract services, trade associations and professional societies.

- *Million Dollar Directory* (Dun & Bradstreet Information Services, Murray Hill, N.J.). In the five-volume version you can find information on 160,000 public and private companies. A condensed version offers information on 50,000 companies. Indexed by both geography and industry, the volumes list parent companies, officers, number of employees and sales volume.

- *The National Directory of Addresses and Telephone Numbers* (Omnigraphics, Inc., Detroit, Mich.). A good source of information once the interviews start because besides information on 137,000 major corporations (including phone, fax, e-mail and Web site listings), it adds special sections that list telephone numbers and addresses for banks, hotels and colleges in 50 U.S. states.

- *Reference Book of Corporate Managements* (Dun & Bradstreet Information Services, Murray Hill, N.J.). Flesh out your research from this directory's biographical profiles of 200,000 officers and some 12,000 U.S. companies.

- *Standard & Poor's Register of Corporations, Directors and Executives* (Standard & Poor's, New York, N.Y.). Lists more than 55,000 public and private U.S. and some Canadian companies with information on products, number of employees, officers and directors. The second of the three volumes has biographical sketches of more than 70,000 key executives.

- *Thomas' Register of American Manufacturers* (Thomas Publishing Co., New York, N.Y.). Another multi-volume (30) study of American corporations. This one has information on 153,000 manufacturers, their products and services.

- *Ward's Business Directory* (Information Access Company, Belmont, Cal.). Data here is organized geographically and alphabetically. The three volumes detail 120,000 companies, most of them privately held.

- *Who's Who in America* (Reed Reference Publishing, New Providence, N.J.). Here you find profiles of more than 92,000 of the country's leaders in business, art, diplomacy, science, education, and so on.

- *Who's Who in Finance & Industry* (Reed Reference Publishing, New Providence, N.J.). The same style as the preceding guide, but with the focus narrowed to 25,000 decision makers in banking, insurance, major corporations, and so on.

It's never too soon to get acquainted with a reference librarian.

cellular phones. The company is famous for cellular phones of the highest quality that are among the lightest in the world. That's key, you'll know from your research, because that's where the growth in cellular phones is— ever lighter, fit-in-your-pocket products. You should also know the radio in the police patrol car that just cruised by is no doubt a Motorola; the company dominates that market. If you want to talk about Intel in the interview, know that's the giant that Motorola intends to do battle with in the semiconductor market.

What to Look for at the Library

Just as when you were a student, the library will be your greatest source of information. If you haven't been in one for more than a novel or two lately, you will discover in many that the computer has made research much faster. Where once you relied solely on the *Reader's Guide* or a newspaper's index, you'll be asking Lexis and Nexis to do the hunting. These two data services for a charge pull stories from a host of sources like magazines, newspapers and the wire services. With the press of a button, you receive printouts you can take home.

If you've ever been frustrated by missing pages or whole volumes lost, these retrieval services are superb and worth the cost. Nevertheless, you should monitor expenses as you go. It is easy to run a $100 tab on the service and end up with handfuls of printouts you might not use.

If your own public library is small, or lacking the kind of resources you'll find described in this chapter, try the nearest college or university library. Often these are open to the public. You start your search in the reference department. Here you'll find several business publications that will give you concrete information on your target firm. Many libraries, in addition to the familiar indexes of periodicals, offer Nexis, the electronic information retrieval service mentioned earlier; its companion, Lexis, is dedicated to finding legal information. It's thorough, fast and neat, supplying you with a printout of the articles you want to see in a matter of minutes. But it costs money, so be mindful of the time you're on the system.

If your library doesn't offer these services, or you don't want to spend the money, you can use the *Reader's Guide to Periodical Literature* to find articles in magazines such as *Business Week, Barron's* and *Forbes*. Major newspapers such as *The Wall Street Journal, The New York Times, The Washington Post* and *USA Today* index their issues. Most libraries have at least *The New York Times* on microfilm.

Many periodicals also maintain Web sites on the Internet. *Kiplinger's Personal Finance Magazine,* for instance, can be reached at http://www.kiplinger.com. There you can search the magazine's archives for information on many companies.

Go by the Book

Don't overlook business books. Big companies are often profiled in book-length studies that can provide an in-depth background on companies you are really interested in (skip this level of research on companies down your list of prospects). *Prophets in the Dark,* by David Kearns and David Nadler (Harper Business; check your local library) details Xerox's rebirth as serious competition to the Japanese in the photocopier business. *Hard Landing,* by Thomas Petzinger, Jr., (Times Business) is a thorough study of the airline industry suitable for anyone seeking a career in that field.

Gather Names

As you read, troll for names and take notes. You'll cross-check each name for spelling and accuracy of the accompanying title with several of the references mentioned later in this chapter. A name isn't necessarily network material yet. But someone you know may know someone who works at the same company as the person whose name you've gleaned. Look for links, memberships you see noted in *Who's Who in America,* that sort of thing. If you're reading profiles, at some point they will get personal. You'll see the boss likes golf, hates to fly, loves trains, is a physical fitness

Start thinking about where you'd like to relocate—or be willing to go for the right offer.

nut. While you may not be interviewing at the top, you'll find fewer pudgy people in a place where the president stays trim and fit. What shape are you in?

You may also discover things about some companies that you *don't* want to talk about in a job interview. The founder's father killed his mother and then himself. (This is true in one major U.S. corporation.) Not that you're going to be cracking tasteless jokes, but you should consider the topics of murders and suicides to be avoided at all cost. A more mundane example would be the company's failures. You can respond when the topic comes up, but you'll know not to ask, "Whatever happened to?"

Will You Need to Relocate?

You may be looking outside your hometown, especially if you're in a highly specialized business or your company dominates your town. (In fact, relocation may be the primary reason for your job search. You may be tired of shoveling snow or the two-hour commute, for example.) Whatever the reason you're looking for a change of scenery, make some preliminary decisions about where you'd like to be—or be willing to go for the right offer.

An important element in that decision is the cost of living in each of the places you're thinking about compared

Small Company Sources

- **Prodigy, America Online, CompuServe, Internet and the like.** Besides the other services they provide, these on-line services are electronic bulletin-board beehives of active job-seekers trolling for information and exchanging information on job leads. You can subscribe to any of these services for at-home use.

- **Business America On-line** (402–593–4593) has a file on small business and high growth companies (often smaller firms) sorted by industry, number of employ-

ees, revenue, or zip code. The list is updated monthly

- **Orbit** (800–955–0906). This company provides a database of over 35,000 high-tech companies that is updated quarterly.

- **The Red Chip Review** (503–241–1265) publishes comprehensive reports on hundreds of small companies. A four-week trial subscription is $49, but check your local library first. Annual subscriptions are $349.

with where you are now. One good source for cost-of-living estimates is *Places Rated Almanac* (Macmillan Travel), which compares costs in all 343 metropolitan areas in the U.S. The book also offers information on education, crime rates, recreation and climate to help you measure cities against one another.

Either way, our test search shows that the homework you do is critical to both pinpointing and assessing opportunities. The box on page 164 lists a variety of broad-based general resources for learning about many different companies. But there are more, many tailored to the specific company, industry or region in which you're interested.

The right job in a small company means much more research is required than when you check out a larger, well-established firm.

Hunting Leads in Small Companies

With 160,000 entries in some research volumes, you'll be covering much of what moves in large and medium-sized companies. But how do you track down the smaller high tech firm that wants your accounting experience? Or find the growing trucking company that needs your skills managing the fleet? Or determine that the little company you thought could, can't, is on rocky financial ground and not worth the risk? Linda Resnick, founder of CEO Resources, a Wallingford, Pa., executive search firm that specializes in finding executives for small firms, ranks three key ways to find small company job leads.

- **Go to your own network,** targeting those people you know who may be involved with small businesses. A buyer at a corporation in the 1990s probably knows about dozens of small companies, what they do, how well they do it, who is in charge.

- **Cultivate people who have dealings with small business** who would profit from a job referral. An accountant you contact tells you, a sales rep, about a small company with an opening that might be perfect for you. You make contact, get a job, and, hopefully, remember the accountant whenever you hear that someone needs help with the books.

- **Join associations, clubs, councils, any gathering** that mixes you with small-business owners. Check out the local Chamber of Commerce for leads on small-business associations and small-business development centers. The National Association of Women Business Owners (301–608–2590) is a good source of information on small, woman-owned businesses, for example.

Job leads are the beginning. Resnick says finding the right job in a small company means much more research is required than when you check out a larger, well-established firm. One way is to track leads back from the company. Who are the principals? Run their names through any of the directories listed above that apply, especially if you have access to any older volumes. *Who's Who*, for instance, or the *Million Dollar Directory* are places to look. Ask the Better Business Bureau where the company is located for information about the firm. BBB can tell you about complaints it has received regarding the company's products or practices. Comb the company's hometown newspaper for stories about the principals, their venture, when it was launched and how it has done since. Check for stories about the company or its principals in your daily newspaper reading.

Networking: Time on the Links

I t's music to your ears. "I'll put in a good word for you. She knows someone. She's got connections. She knows the person doing the hiring." You have a network of people with information on jobs, a few key people willing to vouch for you. Networking can all but guarantee you offers. And yet networking may be the most neglected aspect of the job hunt. It's too bad, because networking is so much easier and more rewarding than stuffing envelopes and licking stamps. Indeed, it's estimated that between 70% and 80% of the job openings available at any given moment will be filled from networking.

What Is Networking?

A popular tune half a century ago quipped about someone who "danced with someone who danced with someone who danced with the Prince of Wales." That's what networking is. Knowing someone who knows someone. Want to make a strong impression in an interview? Know someone she knows and respects. Already you've shed some of your status as an unknown. That's because a cardinal rule of the workplace is that employers would rather hire someone they know than a stranger.

That's why you go *dancing* when you're looking for a new job. Dance with someone and you may have, at least

Remember, you aren't going to ask these people for a job. You're going to ask them about jobs.

indirectly, danced with a Prince. And if the Prince is hiring, you, like the author of that wistful message, will be thinking long and hard about how to contact all the "someones" in between.

Networking was always there—any Southerner in politics or anyone with an Ivy League degree can tell you a story or two, even about themselves, to illustrate the value. So can a New York ward boss or Hollywood cameraperson or a truck driver in Chicago. Whether they called it networking or not, the practice is the same. You know someone, you use that connection to better your situation.

Getting Started

A favorite question at Washington, D.C., dinner parties, one offered with more seriousness than anyone would care to admit, is "Whom do you know?"

In a city that thrives on information and grasps for the power that comes from connections, who you know is critical. You may not admire Washington ways, but the question is the starting point for your network. List everyone you know, categorizing them as:

- friends;

- acquaintances;

- colleagues;

- those with professional positions senior to yours;

- those people you know in other companies or professional associations;

- everyone with whom you do business—vendors, salespersons, ad agencies, public relations firms;

- religious and civic organizations, your pastor, rabbi or priest, the people you meet on any boards on which you serve, the people with whom you volunteer your time at a hospital or clinic; and

- the other people on the panel you chaired at the conference in Denver, for example.

Make a list, and don't eliminate anyone. Remember, you aren't going to ask these people for a job. Not most of them anyway. But you are going to ask them about jobs, and about people they know who might know about jobs in which you'd be interested or who work for companies you want to know more about.

How Other People Do It

Cary Feron, a book editor, can all but take her network for granted. In more than a decade in publishing, she cultivated dozens of contacts that she knows she could turn to if she had to change jobs. How? First, she stayed in touch with those people she met in her first job search, telling them how she was doing, inquiring about the progress of their own careers.

She made new contacts at conferences and other gatherings that would draw her peers and those in the ranks above her. Her network became so effective it began to serve her without prompting. She has turned down job offers that came unsolicited from rival publishers. But, she quickly points out, not in a way to burn any bridge. Publishing, like so many fields, has been the scene of mergers, consolidations and downsizings that tightened an already competitive job market.

"Thanks for inviting me. I can use the exposure."

Steiner, Cartoonists & Writers Syndicate

Ms. Feron's experience highlights a key of networking. It doesn't stop with people you know, it begins there. That's because you're asking each of your contacts to give you the names of others who might be able to get you leads on jobs. Your network's growth is not linear, it is geometric. Two becomes four and four becomes eight, as each contact in turn supplies you with more contacts until it is the vocational

The degree to which you groom your network is up to you. For every aggressive networker who succeeded, there is one who alienated.

equivalent of a chain letter. This one, however, brims with opportunity and remains an asset as long as you nurture it. Lest you think it yields only professional advantage, friendships and more can spring from contacts you make in your work life.

For Vic Mills, a long and distinguished career at Procter & Gamble began from a single contact. A professor at the University of Washington in Seattle was great friends with a vice president at the Cincinnati soap maker's headquarters. He liked Vic, saw potential in the young man majoring in chemical engineering and put in a word for him. In a 36-year career, Vic Mills helped develop everything from Jif peanut butter to Pringles potato chips and Pampers disposable diapers.

Network Your Own Way

Everyone has a network—several in fact. For some, however, the network is a ragtag assemblage of acquaintances who may or may not be entrusted with playing a part in arranging your future. Others, more sophisticated and knowledgeable, have carefully managed their contacts through the years, understanding the value of well-maintained professional relationships.

If you find the latter somewhat calculating, you may be right. On a practical level, it does reflect the values of the workplace and the recognition that success on the job is more than mere competence for the task at hand. How you fit into an organization is often as critical as, and can be even more critical than, how well you do the work. An effective network may yield references as well as job leads as the people you have stayed in contact with decide to suggest your name for positions they may learn about. This may not be your primary goal in networking, but it is an attractive byproduct.

Networking does not mean the surrender of your moral values. The degree to which you groom it is up to you. For every aggressive networker who succeeded, there is one who alienated. Corporate culture, which we discussed earlier in Chapter 8, varies broadly from company to company. Your style of networking will reflect the culture in which you succeed best. Hence, where it succeeds you are more likely to be successful.

Opportunity Is All Around

Networking does not just involve making formal contact with people you know and the people they, in turn, direct you to. It often occurs unexpectedly and can happen anywhere.

For example, Anne Boe, who turned a talent for networking into a career preaching its virtues, likes to prove her point with a story of what happened to her at a seminar on networking. When she discovered she had forgotten an important paper, she left one session to return to her room to fetch it. Never one to miss opportunity, she introduced herself to a man on the elevator who was also attending the seminar. They talked about networking and about her public speaking. He was an executive with a speakers' bureau, an organization that represents colleges and other institutions looking for guest speakers. The linkage is vital to people promoting themselves as paid public speakers. A bureau's annual conventions include a parade of hopefuls giving capsule speeches in a "short-sell" attempt at snagging some bookings. As you may already surmise, the introduction in the elevator led to an invitation to speak at the convention. That led to more bookings.

Anne Boe's forwardness wasn't misinterpreted. She made it plain she was being cordial and communicative. But she had a purpose and she made no bones by disguising it. Her purpose was to make contact—this was, after all, a seminar on networking. Your own foray into this field should be conducted in the same spirit.

There Are Drawbacks

Of course, networking isn't perfect.

It takes time.

Each personal visit can consume an hour or more of time, and if you're still working at your present job

Don't limit your networking to those you know who could help. Use your network to lead you to more names.

you may be doing it during your lunch break or using annual leave.

Networking isn't confidential.

You may wish to be more selective with whom you talk when you are looking if you are still employed. Whatever your status, you should keep your professional network in top shape. Too many middle managers, blind-sided by a cutback in their division, have been left to scramble when they neglected their network of colleagues and professional contacts.

Networking doesn't work as well over long distances.

That means that if you wanted a change of scenery as well as work, networking is not going to be as effective. In the same vein, it is scattershot, leading you here and there, another drawback if you've targeted a city or region, for example, where you want to go.

More Than a Personal Who's Who

It's easy enough to create a file of names and telephone numbers of everyone you've met along the way or to keep a list of people you think could help you find a job. But don't limit your networking to those you know who could help. Use your network to lead you to more names.

DILBERT reprinted by permission of United Feature Syndicate, Inc.

Few people could possibly do it better than Tony Keyes, vice president of a Columbia, Maryland firm that makes telecommunications equipment. Keyes meets many people in his work selling his company's products to the federal government. He makes a point of getting names and numbers from them—mostly in the form of business cards that go into his Rolodex. He tells them to call if they need anything that he can help them with. Many apparently do because Keyes has helped countless of them with leads on contracts, and especially jobs. They in turn have helped him. He credits one $5 million contract to networking alone. Today there are more than 1,000 cards in Keyes' files, every one of them someone Keyes has made contact with, many of whom owe him a favor in return.

"I do it for two reasons," he explains. "First, it makes me feel good to help people. And second, I have a network of people I can call on for help when I need it. And this business runs on networking."

Fine-Tuning Your Approach

Your universe of names may not reach Keyes' four-figure size, but no matter what, it should be divided into several categories (but in any case should be painstakingly accurate with correctly spelled names, titles and telephone numbers). There are those you know, some better than others, nodding acquaintances, perhaps, or people on the other end of a telephone line. Your first networking

Start by working back for at least two months, sending letters to everyone you've had contact with in the course of your work.

contact with them can vary on a spectrum from informal and candid discussions of what you're looking for to less revealing inquiries about the professional lay of the land, for example, or the machinations of a recent reorganization. How much you say depends on how far along you are in your job search, whether you are employed or not and, of course, with whom you are talking.

Then there are those who should probably be categorized as people you "know of." You may find more success in having acquaintances, colleagues or friends closer to these people do the introducing. If you do the calling, keep it light and undemanding (we'll talk more about this later in the chapter).

Finally, there are people you ought to know. This is the most sophisticated tier of networking. Here you become discriminating and specialized, you move beyond "any and everyone" networking. You will have to work the hardest to gain access to many of these people. However, the professional rewards can be great. We'll tell you next how to woo these and other helpful folks to your network.

Strengthening the Network

If your network is looking a little tattered or thin, you can spend some time building up a stock of names in several ways. You begin this foray with simple courtesy and with a practice you should continue until the day you retire—at least. Write follow-up letters. Call them what you will: thank you notes, acknowledgments, birthday cards, whatever. These messages are especially important if you are still working and only beginning your search or if you are striking out on your own and want to be sure everyone knows about it.

Start by working back for at least two months, sending letters to everyone you've had contact with in the course of your work. The "hook," your reason for writing, must be thought out carefully. Your motives, especially if you're going out on your own, need not be hidden, but humor and a subtle message rarely offend.

To help you find an angle for those contacts you don't know very well, consider these points:

continued on page 176

Nancy Franklin: Networking

How valuable is networking? Ask Nancy Franklin of San Francisco and you'll get your answer from one fact: Once she had her first job she never used a resume to find another. That's not to argue against resumes. You need one for a variety of reasons we outline in chapter 7. The point is a network is such a powerful tool it's possible to find jobs solely by tapping it.

Franklin, in her late 40s, moved to Colorado from Virginia after getting a teaching degree. Three years later she stopped to start a family. Once her two children were old enough, she returned to school and received an MBA from the University of Denver. While there, she was a graduate assistant in the marketing department and worked part-time for a professor who also ran a marketing research firm.

The work gave her experience with focus groups and soon she had her own clients, among them the mortgage division of a national home builder. The company liked her work and asked her to shape up its management information systems department prior to spinning it off as a software subsidiary.

One of the women she worked for at the builder moved on to Citicorp in St. Louis and soon called Franklin to join Citicorp, marketing mortgages from the company's San Francisco office.

A downsizing that cost her her job a year or so later barely tripped her stride when the professor she worked for as a student became dean of the business school. He wanted to develop a training program and brought Franklin back to market it. Eventually she was asked to manage it. A new dean took over and asked Franklin to take over as director of student services at the college, a job she held for several years. In the meantime her friend from the home builder who went on to Citicorp had moved on to a large San Francisco banking company. It wasn't long before Franklin got yet another call for a field marketing job.

"I really liked what I had done at Citicorp, and I could relocate," says Franklin. So off she went.

All these opportunities came from networking. It wasn't just that Franklin is a skilled marketing professional. She says the key was that she stayed in touch with many former colleagues.

"Just because the job ends, the relationship doesn't," she explains. "From each place I worked there is a core group of people I keep in contact with. I always know how to get in touch with them."

To keep in touch, Franklin has dinner with former colleagues at least several times a year as her travel schedule allows. She's a big advocate of business networks.

Hers isn't a big list, Franklin cautions. Nor is it a data bank of contacts, but genuine business friends, as she calls them. "There's a finite number of relationships I can maintain. If I were to move from this job, there are two or three people from here that would be on the list, and that seems to be the limit for each job."

"The network is right under your feet," she adds. "No matter where you are or what you're doing, there is a seed for it. If you are in any kind of job, there have to be some people in that job whom you respect professionally and personally. Don't lose touch with those people. And don't shut the door on the first people you worked with. Those people will move up and out and around."

Here's your chance to get an audience with the boss—to be looked over without being passed over.

The easiest reason for writing is probably to ask, why did you meet? Whatever drew you together, unless it was an arraignment, is grounds for at least one letter, even if you're just reviewing what happened. You can use it to promote the notion of a second meeting, there to discuss your career, among other things.

If you've had fairly formal but repeated contact with someone, you might propose a less formal lunch to discuss your mutual interests. Almost everyone enjoys talking shop.

You may also introduce yourself to people with whom you know you have shared interests, albeit unexpressed. For example, you worked on a political campaign or with a group involved with a public issue. Among your fellow volunteers was someone you now want to meet. Your letter can begin with this common ground, suggest lunch or a meeting and go from there.

You'll set the agenda for these meetings, but you can keep it loose. You can talk about your career, but don't ask for career advice, at least not in bald terms. You're making a *contact* here, not a contract. There's a world beyond your work and most of these people are in it. Stick to those topics—dance with the one who brought you.

One cardinal rule never to break is don't overuse someone's name or overstate your relationship. The people in your network, if they are worthy of inclusion, are undoubtedly busy and protective of their own good reputations. If you say you're old buddies when you're not, you could lose *both* contacts.

Informational Interviews

Once, probably too long ago for anyone alive now to remember, someone asked for an informational interview and meant it. You won't find many people today who expect that to be the outcome of any informational interviews they agree to. Informational interviews have been abused to the point where an executive with the time for them probably isn't worth talking to.

Still, as a networking tool, an informational interview is useful. What it has become—now that any job seeker should be able to research any good-sized company, publicly or privately owned, without bothering its boss for details—is a chance to have a non-job job interview.

You lower the stakes, and the expectations, and you limit the time. You get an introduction from someone else in your network to help you get past the front lobby. You agree to keep your remarks brief and not beg for work.

What you get in return is an audience with the boss. You get looked over without being passed over. You get the best of both worlds, a chance to network, to pick up information about jobs in other companies, or this company's plans for hiring in the future, and a chance at anything that's open right then that you may not have known about. Most companies, even those with hiring freezes, are loathe to pass on the opportunity to hire someone they think they need or who would be suitable for a position they know is hard to fill. You also get combat experience on an actual field of battle. You'll find any interviewing you can do will only hone your skills.

Setting It Up

Such precious moments must be carefully arranged. To guard against misunderstandings, you may find it is better to have your contact make the first move. Protocol in these instances means you can't push the matter; if your networking contact is reluctant to speak on your behalf, you'd better rethink what you want. A lukewarm endorsement can be worse than no endorsement. Better to find someone else more enthusiastic to your cause.

After the first move has been made, you follow up with a letter and a call. Remember, you're not on a job interview. You are on an informational interview, trying to establish some rapport with a person who, if he or she is worth any value as a contact, is busy and probably wary of your intentions. Don't confirm those suspicions with a pitch for a job. Your letter should quickly establish the link between you, your network contact and the person to whom you are writing ("Joan Barron spoke with you recently about me") and ask for a meeting at their convenience. Add that you

You're trying to establish rapport with a person who is busy and probably wary. Don't confirm those suspicions with a pitch for a job.

continued on page 179

Networking Letter

Dana P. Williams
2 Park Street
Martinsburg, MO 40513
305-555-1243

June 7, 1997

Karen Walters, President
Jones Valve and Toggle Corp.
12 State Street
St. Louis, MO 63133

Dear Ms. Walters:

Maynard Fahs suggested that I write to you. We've been friends for many years, going back to our days at Detroit University.

For some time I've been considering a shift in the focus of my career. I want to move it closer to our customers. I enjoy meeting with people and I like the concept of promoting ideas and products. In our conversations, Maynard said you would be the perfect person with whom to discuss my interests. So I'm writing to ask for an informal meeting where we might talk about public relations. I know how busy you are, so I won't take more than a few minutes of your time.

With that goal in mind, I will call your office next week to see if we can set up something.

Sincerely,

Dana P. Williams

will follow up with a call to confirm whatever time they set. (For a sample networking letter, see page 178.)

Keep It Brief

The meeting should be short, probably no more than 15 or 20 minutes. Know what you want to talk about before you go. That means researching the company, its products and performance and its plans for the future. Find out what you can about the person you will be meeting, but be discreet with your information when you talk. You want to sound informed, not interrogatory.

Sometimes a moment or two of poker-faced ignorance will help get your networker past what you both realize was an awkward or embarrassing time. For example, you are discussing the brilliance the company showed in dumping an unprofitable line. It was a smart move, but the person you're talking to was in charge at the end—and still smarting over his inability to turn that division around.

An outline sketched on a pad of paper you bring along can serve to prompt you as the two of you chat. Ask if you can take notes. Your interviewee may be flattered—or consider it rude, so be sure you have permission before you start. Have a question or two ready in case you encounter a moment of awkward silence.

And study your surroundings. You're on a research mission to decipher a company. You also want to know about this manager's style so you can decide what to say and how to act. A manager who is willing to shoot the breeze for a few moments conducts business differently from one who takes calls while you're there or moves immediately to the business of answering your questions. If you see something in the office that strikes a chord with you—a school memento, a fishing trophy—you can use that to warm the proceedings. You can also gauge just where this manager falls on the friendly scale by how much response you get. Some managers can't surrender the notion that this is really some sort of job interview, so you may encounter stiffness at first. Again, it is a challenge for you to overcome but evidence, too, of the management style you'd be living under if you came to work there.

When your meeting is finished, end it. Don't wait to be dismissed.

When your meeting is finished, end it. Don't linger waiting to be dismissed. You are in charge of getting yourself on and off the stage as expeditiously as possible. You've made whatever impression you are going to make. Your respect for your networker's time and your skill at directing matters will count highly in your favor.

Following Up

Follow the meeting with a brief thank you note, sent no more than one or two days later. To further refine your networking skills, consider how you might help your new contact. In your research and talk, you may have discovered your contact loves exotic coffee. You know a company that roasts the day it ships. Send on the name and address to your contact. (But don't send the coffee. You're not that close, and so it would look too much like a gratuity, a little bribe or a petty reward for the meeting.) Also write thank-you notes to the people who put you in touch with your new contact. Ask them to let you know if they hear anything about the impression you made.

"The mustard stains on your resume match those on your shirt. I like a man who's consistent!"

Schwadron, Cartoonists & Writers Syndicate

Maintain Good Files and Stay in Touch

No matter how you make a network contact—whether it's someone you've known for years or one you meet in an informational interview—set up and maintain a clear reference file to keep track of your communications with each contact. The type of file you keep is a matter of personal preference. Some people like a notebook, with its large pages available to record a lot of information on a single page for easy review. Others opt for index cards of varying sizes.

Whatever method you choose, record the contact's name, address, phone number and title, and who directed you to them (a useful cross reference). Note when you met and summarize the conversation, including your impressions of the person's style, the culture of the office and any personal revelations that might prove useful as a reason for future communication. Record all names this person gives you.

Subsequent contact with people you meet through networking requires some finesse. You can't just call and shoot the breeze; that's insulting to them. As with the first visit, you must offer a reason for your contact. Fresh coffee? That's a possibility, but it would be more creative to find a fresh angle. The fishing angle, perhaps, or if you share home states, some news from there in the form of a newspaper clipping.

If you believe the person is critical to your search, you could contact your initial go-between and suggest a get-together where you both meet again. A dinner party or box seats at a ballgame are two good possibilities. The attitude on these follow-up meetings is to keep the pressure off. The go-between's presence gives you both neutral ground from which to make more contact, yet not be stuck face-to-face with too little to say.

Another method of keeping in touch is to send an occasional progress report—especially if the contact asks to be kept up with your search. That person might not know of something when you first meet, but might hear about an opening a month or two later.

Remember to keep your file up to date. Place a copy of any correspondence or a dated summary of future conversations in the file. Three weeks later, when your memory will have faded, the file will be there to remind you.

And three years from now, although you hopefully won't be looking for a job, you may find that contacts you made during your search can be helpful in doing business—and you may be able to help them. Maintain contacts, at least with your best sources, even if you're delighted with your new position—you won't want to be in the same position again!

Send an occasional progress report in hopes your contact may hear of something later on.

Handling
Headhunters

The letters carry an air of importance, the phone calls a confident swagger. A confidential search is in progress for an especially talented person with rare corporate skills. The salary is high, the position powerful. Are you interested?

It's a form of flattery, at least on its face, to be recruited by a headhunter. Many people measure their marketability by how many queries they receive each year. Others list who's calling on their resumes, believing that says something about them. Actually, it says a lot, or maybe nothing, depending on *who* is doing the hunting. Some headhunters are paid a percentage of the salary of the position they are filling while others work on what amounts to an hourly wage under a long-term contract for a corporation. You should know the difference, especially if you are not employed, before you become enmeshed in the networks of headhunters and agencies. That's because your job status may affect how you are treated by each group. Consequently, your relationship with them will be ambivalent.

Even in ideal situations where you're a hot candidate and they've got a perfect opportunity for you, your interests and those of recruiters of either stripe are not always going to match. To help you understand recruiters, let's look at how they do business.

Contingency or Retainer?

The days when the job seeker paid a fee to be connected to a job are all but gone. Now, it is almost exclusively the responsibility of employers to foot the bill. With that change, what were formerly "personnel agencies" became "executive search firms" or "management consultants."

Their role grew out of a need for legions of managers following World War II. For the first time, companies realized that rapid growth meant they could no longer rely exclusively on their own ranks for promotions. At the same time the first significant numbers of white-collar workers began shifting jobs in order to advance their careers.

Personnel departments and top management concluded it was more effective and kept better relations with other corporations if a neutral party did their looking—and raiding—for middle- and upper-level positions. Thus the personnel firms became brokers of talent. No longer just clearing houses matching jobs and people, they were now genuine advisors on who "might" be available if the proper offer were made. Conversely, they offered information to job seekers on what "might" be available to the right candidate.

NASA

"I'm sorry, but this job *does* require you to be a rocket scientist. . . ."

From The Wall Street Journal, Permission, Cartoon Features Syndicate

Today there are some 2,800 "headhunter" firms in the United States. Retainer firms, 1,100 in number, fill positions with salaries starting above $75,000 on average. The 1,700 contingency firms search for positions with salaries between $40,000 and $75,000.

But there is a significant division among these headhunters that makes a great deal of difference in how they treat you and how you should respond to them. Some work on a commission, a contingency fee. They are paid only if they deliver a candidate who is hired. Their fee is a percentage of the salary paid the new employee. Others work on a retainer. They are paid a fee, generally an amount equal to a third of the salary being offered, to search for candidates for a specified time. They get their money whether they find someone suitable or not.

That's not to say they aren't under some pressure to deliver. Obviously, a retainer firm wouldn't stay in business for long if it were not successful in finding suitable candidates. To accomplish that, they may work beyond the time set for a search and without further compensation.

Contingency firms are less committed, more content to let a bundle of resumes fall where they will, hoping that at least one or two lands on fertile ground. The hustle for them is not in finding *highly* qualified candidates but in finding job listings they can plug resumes into. Proponents point to their success rate—it is 100% after all, if you count only the ones for which they were paid.

You can't tell by looking which category a firm falls into. Equal numbers of each kind do business in the U.S. Both use the same names and at least on the surface function in a similar manner. They both will accept your resume if you are looking, both will contact you even if you aren't and both keep resumes on file from which they have to fill jobs. One difference is that contingency firms tend to specialize in one or two areas while retainer firms are more generalists. Occasionally each will act in the other's role. Generally, however, retainer firms, because of their somewhat higher status, stick to their method of business. It is only occasionally, or if a firm needs business, that it will slip into a contingency role.

Retainer firms also tend to be involved in searches for senior executives, while contingency firms handle middle-level openings.

The Trouble With Contingency

Why is this so important to you? Think of your experiences with a real estate broker when you sold a home. You two were in a legal partnership that meant the agent got a commission even if you found a buyer on your own. The commission was built into the price—or it came out of your profits. But if you marketed the house yourself, you skipped the commission and probably pocketed more money.

Employers and contingency headhunters work the same way. The recruiter's commission comes if they have submitted your name (generally within the last six months) and you are hired, no matter how you finally made your way to the successful interview. They get paid even if you made what you thought was the first contact. And they get paid, as we noted, an amount equal to as much as 30% or more of your first-year salary. You aren't paying it, but your employer is (and has to negotiate among rival recruitment firms if you've sent several your resume). So when a contingency headhunter contacts you and you agree to let your resume be circulated, you've just added up to 30% to your salary for the first year—in the eyes of a prospective employer. That can be a significant amount of money, especially if you are competing with another candidate who wasn't on any contingency headhunter's list.

That's why contingency headhunters shotgun your resume to as many firms as possible. There are times when you may not mind the added exposure if it leads you to a job. But you force your candidacy through a thicket of intermediaries whose only purpose is to collect a fee for your head. Later in this chapter we'll offer you advice on how to deal with contingency recruiters so you aren't needlessly adding a 30% bounty to your salary requirements.

When you agree to work with a contingency headhunter, you've just added up to 30% to your first-year's salary—in the eyes of a prospective employer.

The Downside of Exclusivity

Retainer firms sprang from somewhat nobler roots. Fast-growing firms needed more talent than they could grow themselves. Wading through all the riffraff that came to them over the transom—from resumes and unemployment lines—took too much time. To streamline the proceedings, retainer firms were created. To make their fees more palatable, they argued they didn't just place ads in the paper—indeed they almost never do—but researched firms and found top prospects before they were even looking for jobs. They went everywhere in their search, rarely specializing in any one field. Then they made the perfect match and everyone was happy.

Sounds great so far, but there are weaknesses in this system, too.

First, a retainer firm has a special and contractual rela-

While retainer firms offer a more substantial link with real and high-level jobs than do most contingency situations, the process is slower.

tionship with a specific company. Contingency firms may come and go, but retainer firms like to maintain a long-term agreement with a client. So while retainer firms are scouring the world for talent, they must at the same time leave their client firms out of the search. No one takes kindly to paying for the services of a recruiter who will in turn rob them of their own talent to serve another client. The rule is that two years must pass after a retainer firm has completed a contract with a company before it can recruit from that company.

A recruitment firm with 1,000 clients has a huge pool of corporations it cannot touch, and yours may be among them. If that's the case, automatically you would not be recruited for a position with any of the recruitment firm's clients, even if an opening seemed perfect for you. You might not even know your company is a client of a retainer firm you contact. With the thousands of resumes that retainer firms receive each year, the majority of applicants never hear any response, let alone one that explains why they are not considered.

Second, if a firm is presenting you as a candidate for a job, it won't shop you around. That's because the business is predicated on the notion that retainer firms are supplying *just* the right candidate for a *specific* position. Remember, they're filling a company's specific need, not trying to find you a job. Once that job is filled, your name may be presented for another position. That could take several months.

As a result, while retainer firms offer a more substantial link with real and high-level jobs than do most contingency situations, the process is slower. Also, if you are unemployed during your search, a retainer firm may automatically place you down the list of candidates.

A Workable Strategy for You

But obviously, there are instances when recruiters perform invaluable work for you and for the employer. There are proper ways to deal with them, both when you don't want to and when you do. One standard procedure, which applies when you're in contact with either type of retainer firm, is to maintain careful records of all your communications. Keep a file on each recruiter you encounter. Include the name of the firm as well as the person you talk with. Note if it's a retainer or contingency firm. Who contacted whom and why? Keep copies of all correspondence and dated summaries of all other communications, whether it's a phone call or in-person interview. As you'll see later, such records may prove invaluable—especially when you're dealing with a contingency recruiter.

Dealing With Contingency Recruiters

As we said earlier, while all recruiters don't work the same way, they often look alike. Your first task in dealing with contingency recruiters is to spot them. They won't deny it, but they may try squirming around the issue if you're not careful.

Conversations that begin with broad discussions of your business and include mention of some recent change in a company you may or may not have heard of are hallmarks of contingency recruiters. They move quickly to you, and want to know whether you would like a shot at the job. If you say yes, or anything approximating yes, and send along a resume, you're theirs for the duration of that job hunt. If they shotgun your resume you could be in for a tangle with other companies you contact, unless you can prove you got there first. (That's where keeping files becomes important.)

Your best bet here is to ask the recruiter if he has a firm and exclusive agreement with the company to send it candidates for a specific job. If he doesn't, tell him you'll represent yourself and end the conversation. Do this whether you made the contact or the recruitment firm contacted you. If the recruiter has no agreement, he is only fishing for resumes to offer freelance to the firm. If you send one you may get a job, but if the hiring firm doesn't want to deal with recruiters or already has an agreement with another recruitment firm, you're more likely to just cut yourself off from consideration at the company for at least six months.

If the recruiter does have an agreement, ask the questions you would of a retainer recruiter (see pages 191 and 192). If you like what you hear, then you can consider sending your resume and getting into the running. But make it clear *in writing* (to protect yourself) that you do not want your resume sent to anyone else or used regarding any other job. You want to keep yourself free of that 30% penalty except when absolutely necessary—that is, for those jobs you didn't know about but would be interested in.

Locating Recruiters

• •

Three good sources of recruiter firm names are *Hunting the Headhunters,* by Diane Cole (Fireside), *Rites of Passage at $100,000+,* by John Lucht, (Viceroy), and *The New Career Makers* by John Sibbald (HarperCollins). Cole's book is a self-described woman's guide to dealing with headhunters; it's out of print but you can look for it at public libraries or used book stores. Lucht is himself an executive recruiter, as is Sibbald. If you want to contact contingency firms, you can find them listed in the Yellow Pages under "Employment Agencies."

Dealing With Retainer Recruiters

They're slow and snobbish. But if a retainer firm finds you a great job with a big boost in pay, you won't have anything but tears of gratitude whenever its name comes up. These recruiters are easier to deal with if they contact you out of the blue. They aren't, at least most of the time, trolling for bodies; they've got an opening and they think you might be the person to fill it. But if you decide you want to deal with them, you'll have to put up with some aloofness when you start.

Ironically, as John Lucht, a leading retainer recruiter in New York City notes, you can tell it's a retainer firm because they won't be half as friendly as a contingency firm when you call on them. Indeed, too warm a welcome is a sure sign you're dealing with a contingency firm or a retainer firm doing a little slumming among the contingencies.

Why are retainers harder to impress? Because they are in the business of delivering the best possible candidate for a specific opening. The chances of you fitting that description at the time you're looking are fairly slim. As a result you'll want to deal with several or as many retainer firms as you can find, remembering that, unlike contingency firms, they rarely specialize in any one industry.

Contacting a retainer recruiter

One way to get into a retainer's office is with a referral, once more calling upon your network to put in a good word for you. Look among your contacts for someone who has done business with a recruiter or who might be likely to. See also the references in the accompanying box.

Composing a cover letter

When *you* contact a recruiter, your cover letter takes what would be in other circumstances the wrong course. Unlike letters to potential employers in which you argue what you can do for them, in this letter you outline succinctly what you have done. Recruiters are looking for a match to an existing opening. They aren't going to spend a lot of time on a cover letter; instead, they'll go to the resume, where they want to see quickly who you are. They don't need speculation from you on how good a job you'd do. And as you can't know what positions they are trying to fill, you can't very well tailor your response. So outline your education, experience and skills, with the intent that your particulars will match some opening. Not the best of situations, but the best you can do under the circumstances. For an example of a letter to a recruiter see page 190. You can use the same letter for both types of recruiters as long as you make it clear to contingency recruiters you are responding to a specific job and no others and don't want your resume circulated.

Managing the interview

If you get an interview, keep it brief and organized. All you're doing is making contact. Expect the meeting to last no more than half an hour. Bring a resume in case the one you sent cannot be located, a common situation you'll encounter in your job search.

You shouldn't expect anything to happen at this meeting. As we noted, the chances of matching you to an

Recruiters are looking for a match to an existing opening. So, in this cover letter you outline succinctly what you have done.

continued on page 191

Recruiter Letter

Dana P. Williams
2 Park Street
Martinsburg, MO 40513
305-555-1243

June 6, 1997

Gordon French
President
Senior Level Recruiters, Inc.
3851 Miramar Lane
La Jolla, CA 92037

Dear Mr. French:

I am writing to you because I am seeking new opportunities for career advancement in information management. Perhaps one of your present or future clients may have an interest in my capabilities.

Since 1982, I have been responsible for all elements of information management at American Amal-Gamators, Inc. in Benson, Mo. For five years prior to that, I was an information-retrieval staff member at Technocratic Applications, Inc. in San Pedro, Cal. I have an M.S. in information systems from Detroit University and a B.A. in medieval literature from Santa Ana (Cal.) State. I am fluent in Spanish, read French and German, and I have traveled extensively in Western Europe and Northern Africa. An enclosed resume further outlines my background.

Should one of your clients need someone with my skills, please contact me. You may call me at my home number listed above.

Thank you for your consideration.

Sincerely,

Dana P. Williams

Enclosure

existing listing are slim. So it's best to deal with retainer firms when you are still employed and if you are just beginning your search. Any other time, when you're in a rush or already out of work, you're not going to be as attractive a candidate. Then, you're more likely to turn to contingency recruiters for work.

When a Recruiter Contacts You

When retainer firms do call, and provided you are looking, you should screen them carefully about the position before you give any information about your interests. You can do this on the telephone or schedule an interview.

- **You want to know what the job is, where it is and how much it pays,** information you should generally receive without debate. Assuming that information makes you interested, ask:

- **To whom would you report, and who would report to you?**

- **What's the atmosphere and culture of the company?** Is this a button-down Ivy League compound or something loose and freewheeling out of the Silicon Valley?

- **Where is the firm in the development cycle?** New with a young bureaucracy and an entrepreneurial orientation, aging and more people-oriented or facing decline?

- **Is it a growing firm, in trouble or just coasting?**

- **What are its goals?** Growth in profits or market share? New product development or an improved service network?

- **And, of course, why is the job open?** Because of layoffs, bloodletting or expansion and promotion?

You'll ask the same questions as in a job interview directly with a company (see Chapter 11). Questions such as starting dates and job responsibilities. Others are more pointed. You still maintain some distance from the job because you don't want to seem too eager. But you can ask about salary, about corporate culture and the like.

If you are not comfortable discussing your pay with strangers, another way is to say what would dislodge you from your present position.

You may or may not be told the identity of the company with the opening. Most times, however, retainer firms do not hesitate to tell you, and if they can't they provide a plausible reason. Contingency firms are more likely to hide the identity of the company, thus avoiding any disputes over how you were led to a given job.

More questions for you to ask the recruiter about the machinations of the hunt:

- **How soon will the decision be made?**

- **How many people are being considered?**

- **Who is involved in the process?** A committee or a department head with full authority?

Such thorough questioning not only supplies you with a lot of information you'll need to make a decision, it also shows how much you understand your business, that you're analytical and you aren't going to jump at something just to get out of where you are.

Discussing salary

What if they ask about money before you do? You can handle that two ways. You can tell them what you're getting, along with any bonuses or options that add to your compensation. They will understand that the hiring company will have to better that to get you to move if you're not looking particularly hard—or at least equal it if you are.

If you're not comfortable discussing your pay with strangers, another way is to say what would dislodge you from your present position. Getting the pay issue up front, one way or another, helps clear the table of offers you might have considered—until you heard what they offered for salary—and saves you both time.

If you have negatives that need to be addressed before any offer is made to you, bring them up now. They can be anything from a serious medical problem in your family for which appropriate health insurance will have to be guaranteed, to stock options that can't be exercised for several months or more.

What to Do When There's Interest

At some point you will either be crossed off the list and communications between you and the recruiter will peter out or you'll become the hunted.

If the latter is the case, then positions reverse. Now the recruiter is working to recruit *you*, not just fill a position. You'll be sent to an interview with the company doing the hiring. The recruiter may be in the room for this and any subsequent meetings up to and sometimes including your negotiations for an employment package. (Contingency recruiters rarely come further than the first round.) The decision to include the recruiter is the client's, not yours. It is very easy at this point to slip into a relationship that has you negotiating with the recruiter. Remember who's paying the recruiter and try to avoid this situation.

"He read, somewhere, that you should dress like the person whose job you want."

Charles Almon © 1996

Mind what you say to a recruiter, too. Your words may be carried back to the client by the recruiter and change the negotiations. As in the negotiating process outlined in Chapter 12, you'll be trying for a win-win situation where both you and the company feel they have done well at the bargaining table.

So order your demands and requirements into priorities (but don't share them with the recruiter). What are the dealbreakers, the minor points, the major points that can be bargained? While you aren't giving away your bottom line, you can outline to the recruiter what you would consider an ideal situation for you. One method of signaling

If you really aren't interested in the job, bail out of the running quickly and offer other appropriate candidates.

the other side you are reaching your dealbreaking point is to narrow the intervals of your decreasing offers. You gave in $5,000 on the bonus; give up $2,000 on the stock option plan. Or even $1,000. You're reaching bedrock on this, watch out, you warn the other side.

In *Stalking the Headhunter* (Bantam), author John Tarrant says you shouldn't be surprised to find a "good cop/bad cop" situation in some recruiter/client negotiations. The client hits the ceiling, the recruiter takes you aside and says there is hope if you would be willing to give in on something else in the offer. It isn't rehearsed but the scenario between the client and recruiter isn't spontaneous either.

Tarrant counsels you to take your time in befriending the recruiter with your confidence. Early on you won't be taken seriously. But when you see that the recruiter's success will depend on whether you take the job or not, then you have leverage you can use to get what you want out of the deal. It is then that you can use the recruiter to send messages to the client about what you can and cannot accept.

You can also use a recruiter to blow off steam if the process is frustrating you. This way you aren't risking the offer with a face-to-face confrontation but you are getting your message across.

If You Don't Want the Position

If you aren't interested in the job but still want to make points with the recruiter for the future, bail out of the running as quickly as you can and offer other candidates you think might be appropriate for the position.

Once you've said "no" that should end you as a candidate for the position. If a recruiter persists, you may have unmasked a desperate retainer recruiter who is acting as if he were a contingency firm. Ethical retainer firms don't have time to cajole.

Effective Interviewing

Your work until now has been for a single purpose—to gain entree to people who can offer you a job. With appointments lined up, it's time to consider the interview, the key to your job search. The stage is set for your act.

And something of an act it should be. An interview is not, after all, a conversation meandering where it will but a structured attempt by an employer to find out who you are and what you have done.

Despite all the talk you may hear from human resources directors about creating an informal, relaxed atmosphere, a job interview is a job interview. You aren't having a bull session with your cronies over a beer, you're checking out a job opening, and the company with the opening is checking you out. The roles are often rigid, one asks and one answers. (At least at first. Later in the interview you should be asking questions as a way to show you've done your homework on the company and the job.)

The footing is unequal, and you're in the weak position. Unlike a regular conversation, it's usually not spontaneous; nor is it open. As a result, you are nervous. You have sweaty palms. You worry about making mistakes, saying something wrong, blowing a sure thing. As if that weren't enough, it turns out they aren't even using the old stock questions anymore. We'll discuss that change later in the chapter.

At the same time, an interview can be an exhilarating experience as you discover new opportunities, learn more about yourself and see how you are perceived in the

An interview can be an exhilarating experience as you discover new opportunities, learn more about yourself and see how you are perceived in the workplace.

workplace. Even the bad ones are good. You find that you don't really want to work at a given company after all. You get practice for the rest of your interviews. Or you see once and for all that your present employer isn't such a bad place after all.

Interviews are useful in another critical way. You get primary research on a company culture, condensed and offered for your consumption. How a company treats prospective employers, how it woos people it wants (and turns away those it doesn't), and how its middle- and upper-level managers conduct themselves and their business can be revelations to the job seeker. It's no small truth that job hunting is as much a search for something you want as a search for someone who wants you.

Different Interviews for Different Purposes

As you may know from participating on the other side of the process, not all interviews are the same, nor are they conducted for the same reasons. Some stops on your way to a job are meant to be exit points, places where you can be jettisoned from the process. Human resources departments tend to fall into this category. They are there to screen the applicants, to reduce the pool of seekers to a manageable size.

Other interviews are there more or less out of a courtesy or to maintain the structure of the organization. You meet your potential boss's boss. She isn't going to make the offer. She isn't even going to overrule the decision of her subordinate. But she wants to meet you before you're hired. Sometimes that's just because it seems more sensible, other times it's because she does want a finger on the pulse of the organization. And there is the off chance that something might happen to reveal an aspect of your background or personality that should be known. You're allergic to a product that's made in the building next to the one where you are working. You've misunderstood that the transfer will be this year, not next, and the company cannot help you sell your home.

For many middle-level positions, you will meet a half dozen people or more, sometimes the whole department where you will work. Top to bottom. Everybody. It can be exhausting in itself, let alone coming while you are under the stress of a job hunt.

You may meet with only one or two people, especially if you are talking to a small organization—and that may be likely if, as with many middle managers in the 1990s, you have been pushed out of a big firm and find yourself scouting opportunities in smaller companies.

What you cannot forget in this process is that each of these people can hold your fate in his or her hands. A bad interview, even with a person outside of the hiring chain, can spell the end of your candidacy. So no matter how confident you have become (and the more interviews you have the more confident you will become), don't drop your guard. You haven't gotten the offer yet.

You'll get primary research on a company culture, condensed and offered for your consumption.

Who's on First?

There's no set pattern of interviews. One company may use its human resources department at the forefront of the hiring process while another may use it at the end merely to explain benefits and process your paperwork. Part of your research should be to determine who does what in a company so you will be better prepared when you interview.

For all the advice to avoid anyone who can't make you an offer, and the subsequent targeting of human resources as the one place to really steer around, you may have to start there. Company policy may dictate that nearly every applicant's resume be screened in personnel before being sent on to a department. This may be a courtesy to the department, but it is more likely a way to reduce the load on busy senior executives. Human resources departments may do as little as match the most promising resumes with the job description, or they may call you in for an interview. Don't be lulled into a false sense of safety, as you will discover if you interview at one major firm.

At Marriott International in Washington, D.C., James Mueller may talk with five or six people a day and send one on to an interview with the department head doing the hiring. His is an exhaustive process critical to almost everyone interested in a middle-level job at the giant food-and-lodging company. You fail in Mueller's office and you had better have an ace up your sleeve if you want to work for Marriott.

"Actually, we're looking for somebody who will be eternally grateful for the job."

From The Wall Street Journal, Permission, Cartoon Features Syndicate

Mueller's style is one you may encounter, particularly at companies with a reputation for sophisticated management and a desire to hire well-screened, highly-qualified candidates. It's not exactly good-cop, bad-cop interviewing—others in the Marriott hiring chain are screening you just as earnestly—but it illustrates how prepared you must be at every point in the process to adapt quickly to changing styles.

What's he looking for? Communication skills for one thing. He wants to see how you act in a setting with a stranger. Nearly every one of Marriott's employees has contact with the public, so it is crucial that you be able to represent the company in an effective way with people you might not necessarily know.

What will you talk about? He won't go over your resume line by line. He's read that already. What he wants to know is how you achieved those goals you touted, or as he quips, "Who did you kill to get there?" He also wants to know your expectations. And he wants to know if you can listen effectively and give answers you've thought through.

"We don't even discuss benefits at the first meeting," he says, dismissing what may be common in other settings. Unlike some companies, Mueller does make the offer and negotiate the employment package. Most times, however, you'll be dealing with your potential boss when you make those moves.

Mueller may not be going over your resume line by line, but you can bet he and most of the people who do serious screening have read it carefully. If he has a question, if he doubts you on a boast of cost reductions, say, of 50% in a year, he'll ask you to explain how you accomplished that. Nuts and bolts. People who listen to people for a living become experts at spotting the lie and the fudge and the embellishment.

If you clear his screening, you'll go on to meet the person who may become your new boss. You'll also spend time with several layers of management. Your experience with them will have more to do with your accomplishments and will be a chance to see if the chemistry between you and the company is good. Here, you won't be explaining who you "killed" so much as how what you did might be applied to the company.

Whether it is personnel or someone else who plays the roles, this bifurcated process may be typical of your experience. There'll be at least one interview where you explain yourself and another where you get to say what you can do for the company. One where your record is on the spot, another where your knowledge of the company is tested.

Both types offer opportunity for you to ask questions. But asking questions is not a goal in itself. You can screw it up and cost yourself points. That's because your questions can reveal much about your understanding of the business you are in and the company you are interviewing with. Questions that merely raise issues already settled or force the interviewer to repeat information aren't going to win you any points. Neither are questions about company history, current performance or other recent events. You should have found that out in your research long before you hung your hat in the hallway to await your date with the interviewer.

Your research must go beyond corporate history and annual reports. You must know the company's products—thoroughly. Eat their ice cream, pump their gasoline into your car, read their magazines, stay in their hotels. Notice the company's branch offices. Check out new products,

Asking questions isn't a goal in itself—revealing your understanding of the company and its business is.

Lunch is a whole different ball game. One false move of the ketchup bottle could turn you into an also-ran.

see if the trucks have been repainted or the slogan has changed. Read the advertising columns in *The Wall Street Journal* and *The New York Times* for news on new ad campaigns—or campaigns that failed—so you'll know what an interviewer is talking about when they allude to a new product, or an end to a jingle everyone had tired of. Check the Internet for web sites that many corporations have established.

Those are kick-off points for questions that will make you shine as a candidate, someone who cared enough to be a customer.

Offers *have* been made at first interviews, but it is more likely that your goal in this meeting will be to get past this round of eliminations and gain a second and subsequent interviews where offers are more commonly extended to winning candidates. You may meet with a single person, with a group or with a series of persons. The more people you talk with the more seriously you are probably being taken as a candidate.

The Etiquette of Interviews

A lot has been written about interviewing techniques, dressing for success, when to schedule interviews, and even the subtleties of body language and placement of chairs. In addition, while you're being examined by a potential employer, the personality and style of the person interviewing you will also be on display, perhaps even more than your own.

Timing Is Important

Try for interviews on Tuesday, Wednesday or Thursday, days that do not come with the built-in disadvantages of the first and last days of the week, with their concomitant start and stop tasks. If you can, schedule interviews in the afternoon, when the day's tasks have already been organized. If you must interview in the morning, try for 10 A.M. rather than 9 A.M., when getting tasks underway may interfere with your appointment. And if you choose 11 A.M. you may end with an invitation to lunch, not as nice a notion as it may sound.

Lunches change the dynamics of the interview process. They open you to another set of tests and another opportunity to be assessed—and eliminated. Why take the chance that your eating habits, choice of entrees or the accidental spill down the front of you will turn you into an also-ran? Lunch isn't very private, either, adding to the stress of answering questions about your past, your work and your goals.

You may, however, have to "do" lunch, especially if you're applying for higher-level jobs. A review of executive etiquette might be helpful. Charlotte Ford's *Book of Modern Manners* (Random House Value Publishing) is a good source of advice. If lunch is unavoidable, order something simple to eat and light like chicken salad, avoiding pastas and soups. Remember what your mother told you: Pay attention to how you hold your eating utensils, where and how you use your napkin and please, don't talk with your mouth full of food, even if the other person does. There's also the matter of liquor. You shouldn't drink, even if your interviewer does, but again, this can create a gulf between you, especially if the second round of drinks really loosens him or her up.

You may, however, have to "do" lunch. A review of executive etiquette might be helpful.

Scouting the Territory

A company's culture will be evident as you make your way to the interview location and again if you interview in an executive's office. You'll get a feel for the place and the people who will be your managers or bosses. Visceral, subliminal feelings are a part of the human senses; don't ignore them.

- **Did the interview start on time or were you delayed because of more pressing business?**

- **Were you greeted personally by the boss or a secretary who ushered you into his or her presence?**

- **First names or Mr. and Ms.?**

Dress as you believe the person you are interviewing will dress, and keep it conservative, modest and in good taste.

- Shirtsleeves or jackets, knotted ties for men or open collars?

- Cluttered desks or sterile clean surfaces?

- Do you shoot the breeze or get right to business?

Remember it all. It will help you evaluate one offer against another, and if you do accept, to make your way smoothly into the corporate culture.

At the same time, the interview is an artificial situation (even more than work) in which, under most circumstances, you will not be seeing people acting as they would with colleagues and employees. Consequently, you'll have to decide how much value to attach to the person who suddenly cradles the back of her head with her hands and leans away from you (she doesn't like what you're saying) or the person who leans forward to be closer to you (you're saying the right thing).

Still, if your answers bring fidgeting or a willingness to respond to distractions, it may be the moment to consider shortening your responses, raising your voice and leaning into the conversation, all proven ways to get yourself back into the limelight. If that fails, and you feel your answers are being ignored because this is the wrong time for this interview, it may be worthwhile to ask if another time might be more appropriate. Your sensitivity and ability to offer a solution to a problem could count in your favor. And you are more likely to have the attention you deserve in the subsequent interview. Of course, a turndown will signal your chance for an offer, at least here, are nil. Best to cut your losses and move on.

Appearance Counts

Your personal appearance and attire *will* be assessed. They speak volumes about your socioeconomic class, taste and sensitivity to the workplace. Just what is said, however, can be subject to interpretation. You can find advice that has you wearing navy blue business suits and other advice suggesting that is too much the "power suit," and you'll be unconsciously threatening to your potential employer.

Better to pick gray, say proponents of the latter philosophy.

Your best bet is to dress as you believe the person you are interviewing will dress. For men and women that now means the same—conservatively, modestly and in good taste—although many women have abandoned the two-piece business suit and selected tasteful dresses and outfits less severe than wool pinstripes. Shirts and blouses commercially laundered, and a fresh press and crease in the suit would be appropriate.

Setting the Mood Once You're There

Try to create a setting in which you are at ease enough to answer questions honestly and completely. Setting the mood starts at the beginning

Barsotti, Cartoonists & Writers Syndicate

with something as basic as the handshake. As sophisticated as we may think we have become, humans still are, well, human. They respond to tactile messages. Your greeting falls into that category. A firm handshake, offered with a smile and eye contact, is mandatory. Practice this maneuver before you do it in an actual setting. You're introduced, you smile, say hello and repeat the person's name. Simultaneously, as you're moving toward one another your hands are becoming aligned for a controlled midair link-up.

Don't trust your spatial instincts. Glance down as your hands meet to make sure you aren't missing one another. More than one person, silly grin on the face, has played what amounted to a vaudeville routine as hands missed one another. This should be a full-length grip, not fingertips to palm or even worse, fingertips to fingertips. Once you're clutching one another, get those eyes back where they belong. This is the time first impressions are made; literally every second counts.

The goal here is not friendship or even professional kinship but a way to an open, free and serious exchange of information.

No more than a couple of shakes ought to seal whatever bond is forming. Break the grip and withdraw your hand. Let the host direct your seating before you move toward a chair. Once you're directed, move to sit down, but let the host settle in before you take a seat.

It's an advantage to you if both of you share the same plane, that is, the interviewer comes from behind the desk and sits in a chair near yours, or the two of you share a sofa/chair arrangement. And if two people are interviewing you, it's to your advantage to maneuver if you can so that you aren't stuck between them. If you are shown a seat between them and sense it is a set up, ask to be seated at one side of both of them so that you talk to both of them at once. Dividing your attention is, you should know, a tactic in adversarial interviews. It keeps you off balance. It also may reveal important information about the culture of the company or the way this manager does business. That's information you'll want to consider as you weigh any offer.

Wait for things to settle before you initiate any conversation. Your host may have last-minute details to arrange or may need to tell the secretary how long you will be meeting or that you two are not to be disturbed. Remember, everything that concentrates attention is good for you and everything that does not is bad.

Whether to initiate small talk is a judgment call for you. Some interviewers are open to a little light banter. It loosens them up too, and gives you a starting point. Other times, you may find your interviewer is a busy, serious person who wants to get right to the point with you. Don't distract him or her with needless banter. But do have something you can comment on if you sense it is appropriate. If you're in a strange city, that can be the monument you saw on the way from the airport, some new building under construction or even the weather, if it's a positive point.

Your goal is to establish rapport. That's not friendship or even professional kinship but a way to an open, free and serious exchange of information. Of course, this doesn't mean you can't be friendly. And don't ignore what are more clues to a company's culture and the style of this particular manager.

Watch How You Answer

While you're interviewing, don't try to take control of the conversation or become hostile or aggressive, even if you are being asked tension-building questions (sometimes a tactic to see how you react under stress). Don't talk too much (see more on this later in the chapter).

And don't interrupt. Cutting off someone a beat or two before the end of a sentence is annoying and rude. And it may be more than that. Sure, you've caught the gist of the question and you want to show off your sharpness with a snappy reply. But wait. Like those on game shows, the question may come with a hook at the end. What if the final phrase, the one you cut off, was "but I don't agree with that"? There you are, nodding away, alone in your endorsement. Also, by being polite and giving yourself that extra beat, the little pause between the question and the appropriate time for you to begin your answer, you give yourself a chance for last-minute reconsideration of your answer. You can also lower your voice, and sound more confident and relaxed and in charge of your answer.

Speak up. Smile when it seems appropriate. While the conversation is serious, it doesn't have to be grim. Show you enjoy the give and take of constructive conversation and your work when you describe it.

Mind Your Body Language

As much as you may be watching body language in the interviewer, be aware of it in yourself. Don't fidget, bite your lip or tap your fingers or a pencil. Keep good posture and lean into the conversation. Bert Decker, a communications expert who has taught 60,000 people how to be more effective in an interview, says the small of your back should be touching the chair back and your upper body should be erect but not rigid. Try to express your energy by gesturing naturally with your upper body. Keep your knees slightly flexed so you could bounce on the balls of your feet.

Some interviewers think tension reveals the real you. About all it usually reveals is the real them.

Don't try to memorize your answers. You just want to sound well-briefed and familiar with the issues.

What If You Don't Like the Interviewer?

Chances are good you'll meet someone who makes your skin crawl. Lucky for you they didn't save this guy for new-employee orientation. Some people take sincere and disgusting pleasure in reliving boot camp whenever there's a job-seeker to interview. Others think tension reveals the real you. About all it reveals in most situations is the real *them* (and again, insight into how the company operates).

Nevertheless, don't become emotionally upset. To compose yourself if you are feeling the heat rise around your collar, you can ask for the question to be re-phrased or you can repeat it—two excellent ways to take the steam out of a contentious situation. But if that doesn't work, better to leave the room or end the interview.

A Little Rehearsal Will Help

With so much riding on how you present yourself in the interview, you should practice interviewing with friends or colleagues. Make the experience a real "dress rehearsal," complete with arranging an office setting and wearing the appropriate clothes. Use a video camera to record your performance. Then you can see yourself as others see you. You can also catch that nervous gesture, the stutters, the fluttering eyes, or the mumble you thought was just measured speech.

Start your rehearsal with your entrance into the office and continue through introductions and seating. Once you're underway, use the questions you'll find later in the chapter and have your "interviewer" ask about specific achievements outlined in your resume.

Try several interviews, with your friends playing several different types of interviewer—from friendly to challenging. You'll learn how to give concise answers to questions you're likely to be asked. Don't try to memorize these answers. You don't want to sound too slick, as if you interviewed for a living. Just well-briefed, someone familiar with the issues on the table, namely your skills and their job prospect. Don't avoid this step, especially if you have been out of the job hunt for any time. Interview skills go stiff fast. If you're out of work and looking, or onto a real find of a job prospect, going into an interview without practice at a time when you're under pressure, can ruin your chances for an offer.

Your Witness, Mr. Mason

Hopefully, your interview won't feel like a trial, but your answers will be judged, and in a sense your fate is in the balance, especially if you're looking at a job you really want. So you want to have the best response to every question. To that end, you've probably thought about your goals and where you want to be and what you like. Stop! Not all of the questions put to you in a job interview will be ones that you have heard, even if you've read books with advice on interview questions. Experienced interviewers have gotten wise, even jaded, to the answers they were hearing to questions.

As Mueller at Marriott likes to do, they're more apt to press a point with you, take a line from your resume, for example, and ask you more about it. How did you reduce overhead by 20%? What projects did you complete there that would make you a better candidate for the job we have?

"I want to know what makes a person tick. If they've been successful at something, I want to know why and how," says Philip Sanborn, now a management consultant in Reading, Mass. In his former role as a human resources director of a Massachusetts high-tech firm, he talked to scores of middle- and upper-level executives. He had some boilerplate questions he had to ask—questions about when a person was available to begin work, salary ranges, would a candidate relocate? But he categorically rejected the most typical of interview questions such as "where do you see yourself in five years?"

That's because the canned questions don't get much beyond the surface—too many outplacement firms, campus recruiting offices and how-to texts have coached

Be prepared for bottom-line questions: What did you accomplish? How much did you save?

too many job applicants with the "proper" answers.

Former campus recruiter, David Magy, all but gags on the thought of asking someone "what's your weakness?"

"Of course they will say they work too hard, or some answer like that," he explains.

So what *will* you hear?

"Bottom line" questions. That's because companies have been downsizing and becoming more competitive. They are looking for people who can make immediate bottom-line contributions.

The best advice to the upper-middle management candidates: Think over what your accomplishments have been and how they benefited your company. "How did you do it and whom did it benefit?" is the tack you should take.

A specific question might be, "How much did you save the company when you tightened procedures in the warehouse? or when you reorganized the sales staff?"

Variations on Three Basic Questions

You'll also hear questions aimed at eliciting answers to three concerns any employer has before an offer is made.

- Can you do the job?

- Will you fit in?

- How much do you want to be paid?

Rather than attempt to memorize some response to a batch of questions you *think* you will be asked, use these three concerns to categorize the questions you are asked. For example,

- **"Can you do the job?"** becomes "How long before you can contribute?" Your answer should be a realistic six to 12 months.

- **"Will you fit in?"** becomes "What is your management style?" Your answer: "Open door." Of course, if it isn't, you should say so. There's no point in setting yourself up by being out of sync with the style of the place you're working.

- **"How much salary?"** The best answer for everyone is you know they will be fair.

  Variations on these themes will play off your resume.

- **"Are you overqualified?"** ("Will you fit in?") Your answer: Strong companies need strong people on board. And emphasize your interest in long-term employment—that says you expect promotions to the rank you should be holding. You can also say that they can expect a fast return on their investment in you because of your experience.

- **"Why are you leaving?"** (Again, "Will you fit in?") You can say you and your boss agreed to disagree or say you want more challenge or say your department is being phased out (if that's true, of course). But don't show much emotion, especially anger, about any of it. You don't want to be branded as a troublemaker or a chronically unhappy person.

All these questions can effectively halt an interview if you don't have an arsenal of appropriate answers on the tip of your tongue.

Some Other Pitfalls

Got something you want to hide? Interviewers say your best approach is, of course, to be honest. Nothing will get you off the hire list faster than a lie. Bluffing, hiding and hesitating are almost as effective in ruining your chances of getting an offer. If you spent six months at home between jobs, say so. But be certain to add what you did in that time that improved your candidacy. You read everything Peter Drucker ever wrote on management, for example, you volunteered in the children's ward at the hospital at Christmas, or you learned to surf the Internet. You want to convey the impression that you don't waste time—and the most precious time you have is your own.

If you've got a black mark on your record—you were fired for cause, you've been convicted of a crime—your best course is to explain what happened and take responsibility

Honesty is the best policy. No bluffing, hiding or hesitating allowed.

An off-limits question may just reflect ignorance. If you otherwise like the company, cope with a light touch that deflects the issue.

for your actions. Critical to getting past this crisis is that you tell the recruiter what you *gained* from the experience. If your problem occurred when you were just starting out, don't hesitate to let youth take some of the blame. Everyone was young once.

If you were the victim of a cutback, merger or your company went down the drain, take heart, the stigma of unemployment from that situation has all but disappeared. It's probable the person interviewing you knows that situation well, if not intimately. Human resources consultant Philip Sanborn, for example, presided over two downsizings at a former employer before he recommended that his own job be phased out.

Questions That Shouldn't Be Asked

If you're asked what you consider to be illegal questions, how do you handle those? The areas off limits today include discussions of your religion, political affiliation, ancestry, national origin, parentage, your birthplace or the naturalization status of your parents, spouse or children. You don't have to answer questions about your native language or the language you speak at home, your age, date of birth or the ages of your children. You can be asked whether you are over 18 years of age, and if you used any other names in prior employment or education.

Questions about your spouse's employment or whether you plan to marry are also taboo. You can deal with these questions by saying you don't believe they're relevant to your ability to do the job or ask the interviewer to explain their relevance. If you like the other aspects of the company, you may just be dealing with ignorance. You can cope with a light touch that deflects the issue. Women may be singled out for questions about their marital status and plans for children. A good-humored response that acknowledges the question without really answering it often works. For example, you're asked about kids. Say your focus now is on your work. You've always thought you would have children, but if you do it will be later. Then get the conversation back on track by asking about the specifics of the job.

If you want to formally complain, ask for a business card from the interviewer and indicate you are filing a complaint with the Equal Employment Opportunity Commission and considering legal action. You might even be offered the job on the spot as a result. It's an offer, however, you would probably be wise to refuse. Would you want to work at a company with tactics like that?

What do you do with the pregnant pause? Wait it out. Dead air cuts both ways.

Testing You

While some of the routine questions may be gone, you may still be subjected to some old-fashioned hiring games.

First, and often scariest, is the stress interview. That's where things go from some degree of cordiality to a purposeful toughness. You get asked questions that are designed to make you nervous, throw you off balance and measure your response to the resulting stress. This is probably used more by recruiters and personnel department representatives whose role is to screen out applicants.

You may also get the third degree if there's a question surrounding some part of your resume. You quit a good job before you had another one, for example.

If you're in a career where stress is a key to the work environment, Wall Street, for example, then even someone empowered to hire you may ask you tough questions about just why you stayed with a failing company or why you took what appeared to be a lateral move. The tone will be unmistakably antagonistic or questioning.

The best course of action is to anticipate this situation and practice answers at home before the interview. Don't get flustered. The interviewer is probably at least as interested in the way you react to the question as to the answer itself.

Then there's the pregnant pause, still an effective tool for many interviewers. Its purpose is to draw you out. You're nervous, you've given them the answer you rehearsed, they've heard it. Now they just sit there silently, betting you'll jump in to fill the dead air and finally give them an honest, unrehearsed answer.

That suits their purpose, but it may not suit yours, depending, of course, on the question. What do you do? Wait them out. Dead air cuts both ways. Your silence may improve your position, and you won't have put your foot in your mouth to do it. If you simply cannot stand the silence then ask if there is anything more the interviewer would like to discuss.

Some Uncanny Answers to Canned Questions

They may be out of style but that doesn't mean they are out of existence. Canned questions will always be lurking in the minds of inexperienced or nervous interviewers. It's a way to keep you talking while they do some thinking.

So you won't be at a loss for words, here are 12 stock questions along with some solid comebacks. You can find more answers in the third edition of *Knock 'Em Dead: The Ultimate Job Seeker's Handbook,* by Martin John Yate (Adams).

Q. *What would you like to be doing five years from now?*

A. Speak to your reputation. Say you'd like to be regarded as a professional and a team player. Say you'd like to be in the part of the company that's growing. Don't say you want the boss's job.

Q. *Have you done the best work you are capable of doing?*

A. Of course you are proud of what you have done, but be sure you say the best is yet to come, or you'll be seen as over the hill.

Q. *How long would you stay with the company?*

A. You can turn this one around and ask how long the interviewer thinks you would be happy with the company. Add too that as long as you were growing professionally there would be no reason to leave.

Q. *What did you dislike about your last job?*

A. The real question is, "Are you going to be trouble?" So say you want to make a greater contribution. Never say anything bad about anything related to your last company.

Q. *How much money do you want?*

A. Tell them what you're earning, that you'd like as much as your background and experience permit, but that you know they will be fair with you.

Q. *Why should I hire you?*

A. Keep your answer short. Highlight the portions of your background that apply to the job opening and end by saying you're qualified, a team player and you take direction.

Five Ways to Blow an Interview

James Challenger, the outplacement expert, says people who blow the Q-and-A section do it five ways:

Saying too much

When they're asked to talk about themselves, they talk too much, and in the process so narrowly define themselves that they're eliminated from the candidate list. Challenger recommends keeping replies general and

Q. *What is your greatest weakness?*

A. It should not be a desire to answer this question. Turn it around, saying you work hard and sometimes are frustrated by those who do not. You overcome this weakness with a positive attitude you hope is infectious.

Q. *Why have you changed jobs so often?*

A. While you're probably settled into a job you've held for some time now, you may have had a flurry of job switches earlier in your career. It is probable your forward progress will make job hopping a moot point, especially now, when cutbacks make job switches more common. But a question you can't answer that highlights perhaps a low point in your career won't do you any favors, so you should have an answer for it. Blame those days on youth or explain how each job was a step up from the last. Call your hopping a chance to experience different situations. You may also say you were underpaid, the commute was too long, you wanted a better company or the job was neither stable enough nor challenging enough to keep you interested in it.

Q. *What did you and your boss disagree about?*

A. Nothing. Nothing at all.

Q. *Are you willing to travel?*

A. Do they mean on Thursday or for the next three years? Ask about the specifics, but finally say "yes" for the time being. Saying "no" can all but end your chances for the job, especially when you consider they are asking you about the issue, proof enough it is a consideration for the job. Obviously, if you can't travel you don't want a job that keeps you on the road, and you wouldn't work out if you took it. But saying "yes" leaves you on the list and open for negotiation.

Q. *What are your long-range goals?*

A. Start your answer with "In a firm such as yours..." rather than "I would like the job you are advertising." With the former, you send a message that you intend to grow and prosper in the firm. The latter says you just need a place to hang your hat.

Q. *What do you like? Dislike?*

A. This is a canned trap question. What's really being asked is: "What are your strengths and weaknesses?" Answer it accordingly.

*Use your thank-you
letter as a
straightforward
way to follow-up on
your oral answers.*

very brief, letting the interviewer lead the conversation to better things. Your answers should probably last at least 20 seconds but no more than two minutes, and don't do more than half the talking during the conversation.

Focusing too narrowly

People are often far too specific when they are asked what they're looking for. "You just talk yourself out of a job by offering the company a product it doesn't want to buy," he says. Stick to general skills so you're selling benefits a company may want.

Talking money too soon

The first interview should pass without mention of money. Don't say what you want until the company makes an offer. Prior to that, just say you know they'll be fair.

Dwelling on the negative

When you're asked why you left the company, don't end up sounding like you were incompetent or you didn't like anyone where you last worked. Don't turn this question into a bull session about work. Instead, be sure what you say is true and that it doesn't make you or the company you worked for look bad.

Baring all

And the uncommon but not unheard of "what are your faults?" question. People get too honest and end up offering a litany of reasons why they shouldn't be hired. Challenger says even canned answers such as, "I worked too hard and my wife hated it," are replies he can live with.

Above all, don't talk too much. "You ask them what time it is," says one corporate staffing manager of the wordy types he doesn't like, "and they tell you how to make a clock."

He's satisfied with an interview when he leaves with a feeling that he's come to know the person. You can measure the success of an interview this way, he says, if in turn you can say afterward, "I understand them and they understand me."

Following Up

Everyone has felt the remorse of realizing "what I should have said." Job interviews are no different. You'll undoubtedly go over your answers repeatedly, especially if you feel you blew the interview or if you really want the job and know your answers can make or break your chances for getting an offer.

You do have a second chance, albeit an abbreviated one, to clean up loose ends or possible misunderstandings. Include any comments you want to add to your oral

Follow-Up Letter

Dana P. Williams
2 Park Street
Martinsburg, MO 40513
305-555-1243

July 2, 1997

Donald P. Johnson
Continental Divide Corp.
9127 Shantz Ave.
Denver, CO 80220

Dear Mr. Johnson:

It was a pleasure meeting with you last Thursday to discuss the director of information systems position in your Boulder facility. The work sounds challenging and especially suited for my background in directing information systems at American Amal-Gamators.

To add to our discussion of cutting costs, I'd like to point out that I reduced turnover to 4% annually in the information systems division, the lowest in the corporation. We both know the high costs of excessive turnover in lost time and training costs.

Again, it was a pleasure meeting with you. I hope we can talk again.

Sincerely,

Dana P. Williams

answers in your follow-up thank-you letter. Introduce these paragraphs in a straightforward manner saying, "to add to our discussion."

Keep your letter brief. More than one page would signal you're doing a lot of second guessing about what you said the first time. Send the letter in the week following your interview and no later. You want to offer a *fresh* reminder of your visit, not something that by its tardiness signals you don't do things promptly. See page 215 for an example of a good follow-up letter.

Add summaries of all interviews to the reference file. Keep track of when you met, what was asked—and your responses—your impressions of the interviewer and the company, and any other information that could prove useful in callback interviews.

Getting It Right This Time

You're poised on the brink of a new beginning. You have the promise of a job offer still ringing in your ears. It's easy in such delightful times to grab the first offer and run with it. You don't have to, and you probably shouldn't. This isn't the time to jump out of the frying pan and into the fire. Remember, this time you are in control and you want to stay in charge. Section Three will help you hammer out the best deal from the offers you're receiving as you near the end of a successful job hunt. You can counteroffer, but you must know the rules or you will sabotage your chances. You can bargain for more than just money—you can negotiate benefits, vacation time, relocation expenses—and not jeopardize your chances. You can deal for the right working conditions to guarantee your success early on in the job.

If getting there is half the fun, staying in charge of your career is the other half, particularly for mid-careerists like you, people looking for a change. In the final chapter of this book, you'll learn how to wend your way through the first critical months of a new job when you make your mark, build your alliances and discover new opportunities.

217

The Offer: When to Say Yes

There comes a moment in the discussions when you realize you are going to be offered a job. The mood changes, the questions seek different information. No longer are you being probed for weaknesses. Now, the inquiry regards when you might be available to begin. Salary and benefit packages suddenly have hard numbers attached. There's too much smiling.

Then the offer appears. Few things in life are as sweet, especially to the unemployed or those dissatisfied with their present position, as someone saying you're the one for the job. There's so much promise—the potential for success is renewed with this most sincere endorsement of your professional efforts. Even those blessed routinely with recruiter feelers or out-of-the-blue calls won't deny the pleasantness of the experience, even when it forces tough decisions later.

Obviously, job offers are what job seekers want. But there's so much to a good one, whether it is said, written or implied. What are your responsibilities going to be? Where are you going to work? Who will work with you? For you? Who will you work for? How much will you be paid? What about perks and benefits?

All these issues must be settled before you give notice where you are and accept a new job. Much of the negotiating you did took place before the offer was made, as you interviewed. The company sensed what you might cost, whether you could carry the sales department as well as marketing, or were willing to relocate to the Tucson office for three years.

In the best situations, you understood each other very well and the offer matches your needs and expectations. If it doesn't, then you must decide whether you want to negotiate or pass on the deal. The latter points to a failure during the process. Either you were misled or you didn't make yourself clear. Assuming you would have wanted the offer under better terms, let's focus on the process before it hit these shoals, a time we'll call the preamble. It's the period before the hard offer is made.

The Preamble

If you could see yourself as others see you. That's an instructive saying few of us can act upon. But let's indulge our imagination this once and look at your situation from the other side. From that vantage point, you're candidate 1-B, the person from Seattle. You were interviewed last Tuesday and Wednesday. You come with a price tag, an aggregate of your salary, bonuses, benefits, payoffs, stock options, special health insurance, moving costs, relocation fees, spouse career assistance, years to retirement and so forth. That's only the base. On top of that, there's what it would take to woo you into the fold. Ten percent above what you are getting? Twenty percent? The cost of buying you out of a stock option? More? Much more?

"Congratulations, Stanley—your promotion came through! From now on, you'll be coming in early, staying late and working during your lunch hour."

From The Wall Street Journal, Permission, Cartoon Features Syndicate

Still, if you're the top candidate, or number two and number one is showing signs of balking at the deal, you're worth the trouble of some bargaining sessions. You're brought to the table. What would it take to get you?

What you must realize is the table you're bargaining on is marked. You don't start at the edge and move to the middle. You start somewhere closer than that. Why? Because in the process of checking you out, of talking with you and perhaps the recruiter who brought you in, the price tag evolved. You weren't a passive player in this. Your words helped them reach their conclusion.

How did you do? Maybe not too good, if what you really want is too far from the offer to make bargaining a profitable experience for either of you. You've got to be positioned long before the offer so that the company you're dealing with understands what you will cost.

Philip Sanborn, the human resources consultant in Reading, Mass., tells of one man, in line for a top financial position in a large, high-tech firm, who blew a solid offer. During his preamble he made a fatal mistake. He low-balled the amount of salary and benefits it would take to get him aboard. Why? To stay in the running, he said later. The company followed his lead and made him an offer it thought he would accept. He waffled and waited.

Sanborn was dispatched for another round of questions. It was then that he got the deal-breaking answer. All along, the guy had wanted more. He thought that when he stalled the company would panic and put more money on the table. And it might have under other conditions, Sanborn said. The company wanted his services, after all. But his tactic raised fatal questions about his integrity.

"We didn't boost the offer because he wasn't up front from the beginning," Sanborn explained. "Integrity is the key issue in today's world. You should say what you honestly feel rather than wasting everyone's time. You just can't win that one."

You and the company need to know up front what you'll cost—no low-balling allowed.

Figuring What You Need

Your "honest feelings" don't come just from your heart. You have to have figures from which to deal. Details about your job, your pay and benefits. Commuting time, schools for your kids, the culture and amenities of the city where you live. The whole fabric of what you have today

Taking stock of your needs goes far beyond just salary and bonuses.

must be measured against any offers. (More about those later in this chapter.)

Even if you are unemployed, you should form an outline of what you want, the amount of compensation you would accept. Most employers know offering you substantially less than you believe you are worth only means that if you accept you're going to keep looking for a job that does pay enough.

Arriving at your own bottom line takes yet more preparation.

Measure your worth.

Measure everything about your current position that you value. Start with the obvious factors such as salary and bonuses. To this add any raises you expect to get, the rewards of a promotion you're in line for in the next year, any plans in which you will be vested in the coming months. Don't overlook the growing profit-sharing plan you'll be cashed out of, especially if there's no like plan where you're headed. Stock option plans must be included if you have them. You may find measuring their value difficult. One method: average the value of the stock for the last three years. If that isn't valid, you can estimate the future value using a forecast of earnings-per-share growth. You can find that information in *Standard & Poor's* or in *Value Line* at your local public library.

Add any unique provisions made for you such as special medical coverage if you or a member of your family has a condition that requires special consideration from a health insurance plan. Company-paid memberships in professional organizations, private clubs or the like also fall into this category. Do you have a company car allowance? How about a company car you can take home at night?

Other factors: The cost of a commute? The use of the company's Florida retreat or Colorado ski condo provided to you at cost or for free? If any of those has significant meaning to you, include it—you'll give it up if you leave.

Consider cost of living.

If you are relocating to another city, your work is compounded. You should have done some basic comparisons of the area even before you applied for a job with the company, as discussed in Chapter 8. Now it's time to get down to details, because the difference in cost of living can wipe out even a hefty pay raise. For example, move to Joplin, Missouri, and a house will cost you half the U.S. average. But take a transfer to San Francisco, and you'll be paying almost *four times* the national average, or almost eight times more than you would in Joplin. That figure alone could break a deal for anyone from the Land of Lincoln who wasn't earning a big salary before and won't be after the move. (Of course, if you're considering a move from San Francisco to Joplin you may be evaluating a compensation package that's less than what you've been earning.)

Costs you might not have considered.

You have to measure the entire cost of change—lost tuition at your kids' school, club memberships that are paid for a year that you will forfeit. The cost of selling your house and buying another is a significant factor. Many firms have provisions to compensate you, even going so far as to guarantee the sale of your old home, but you should know that before you make a final decision. Other cost factors can't be ignored. Annual state and local taxes—or even utility bills—may be significantly higher in San Francisco than in, say, Austin, Texas. Books such as Macmillan Travel's *Places Rated Almanac* will help. Or contact the local Chamber of Commerce in the area you're considering.

The bottom line.

Once you have toted all these figures you have an annual compensation and a baseline figure from which to decide just what it would take to unseat you.

If you are working through a recruiter, make these figures available early in the proceedings—your preamble

Look for the hidden costs of relocating.

And, then there are the non-financial, quality-of-life issues that can make the perfect job much less desirable.

is set this way. You can show your figures to the recruiter or just make them known verbally. That way, the recruiter understands from the start what you're worth and won't underprice you in the market.

In your own dealings with the company, you will probably be asked what you are earning. Be honest if you give a figure. Most employers know they'll have to better that one way or another to get your services. Inflating your salary may push you out of the running for jobs you would like. If your dishonesty is discovered, you've ruined your chances for that job and maybe a number of other opportunities with the company.

You may have to show your earnings for the last three years. Those figures, a kind of earning curve, indicate where you're headed, where you are and sketch in more information about your salary requirements. (They can also reveal where you've been if things are going down hill. If that's the case, be prepared to explain what happened.)

Deal-Breakers

In the course of hunting for a job, it's easy to overlook an important set of factors. Not your salary, not your title, but issues we'll call "deal-breakers." Those are conditions and factors you know you cannot accept. Before you let an almost perfect offer turn your head completely, spend some time considering what you want from your next job. This can be a time to indulge yourself; you'll pour a dose of reality on at the end when you're making your final decision on an offer. But for now, consider those factors such as the size of the city you really like, the climate that suits you best, the amount of cultural life to which you are accustomed.

Anyone who has endured a metropolis when in his or her heart beats the soul of a small-town person, knows what a drag a big city can be with endless lines, endless crimes and sky-high prices. Conversely, a hick town in a backwater state can offer unheard of levels of boredom to someone used to a five-pound Sunday paper, visiting heads of state and a steady stream of nationally known art shows.

Climate is no different. Buffalo may be sensitive about its reputation, but spring just doesn't arrive there as soon as it does in Norfolk, Va. (Of course, neither does the humidity.)

You may have family to consider. Your parents are getting on in years. How far from them do you want to be? Your brothers and sisters have become your closest friends since you moved near enough to visit regularly. Now you want to end that? Life is too short, you may say.

A rule of thumb is that you should pick up at least a 20% gain in your compensation to make a move worth your while.

Your Own Tenure Track

A merger may have thrust you into a new town. Now you realize this round of layoffs is probably going to include you. You want another job lined up, but is this the time to consider a return to your hometown? To the city you and your family started in? Maybe that was a personal debacle and you want a brand new place, one where things will be fresh with no history to haunt you?

To cope with these issues, you may negotiate a tenure for your services in a given city. For example, you could agree to work for the corporation in Cincinnati for three years. Barring any performance problems you will be transferred back to Portland at the end of that time.

Financial matters are no less important, of course. A rule of thumb is that you should pick up at least a 20% gain in your compensation to make a move worthwhile. You may have to throw that rule out the window to join a start-up company with a lot of potential or to land on your feet after a lay-off. But don't forfeit a pay hike in a panic to find a new job. Negotiate for what you think the job is worth to you. That compensates you for the risk you're taking jumping to a new job. That's a rule of thumb you are, of course, free to break (though you may not have to) if you're moving because you want to reduce stress, change your lifestyle or return to your hometown, for example, or because you decide you want to work for a given company no matter what the cost. You can also suspend this rule if your income needs are changing. Your children are through college, you'll be able to sell expensive, big-city real estate and use the money to buy a cheaper home in a smaller city, for instance.

Whatever your calculations, don't leave out a cost-of-living differential. San Francisco, the most expensive place to live in the U.S., according to *The Places Rated Almanac,* is almost three times as expensive as Pine Bluff, Ark., so you should expect to be paid much more to work there than you would if you did the same thing in Pine Bluff.

But even with a cross-town move to similar work, you should receive a significant boost in salary. After all, you are taking a risk that the new job may not work out in a year, or even a few months. You need an incentive to cover you for that.

Measuring the percentage though can involve some maneuvering. You may find you have been offered all a company can give for the position you are seeking. Do you still want the job even though that's not quite enough? You may find you can get rewards in other ways. You could be offered more vacation, for instance, or a bonus in the first year to cover the difference in pay (assuming that your performance in subsequent years will justify a raise to bring you up to what you want). Car and expense allowances are two more sources of income you can negotiate as incentives to move.

To head off a deal-breaking impasse, you may add a severance guarantee tailored specifically for you as a way to enhance the offer. Instead of six months, you'll get a year's pay if you are laid off, for example. Or you can add an up-front signing bonus, a fee to compensate you for your risk.

You can agree that if the company is bought by or merged with another, you will receive specific amounts of severance if you are not retained. This is your own version of the golden parachute.

You may find some of these provisions available only in smaller companies where there are fewer positions like yours, or, if you're in a larger corporation, only for senior management. Large companies tend to shy from compensation programs that are not uniformly applied to middle management because individualized packages can create both morale and legal problems.

Looking at a Specific Offer

Armed with a clear understanding of what you have and what you want, it's time to look at specific offers. To give you time to do this, it's important to forego accepting an offer for at least a few days, and for a week if you believe you can without jeopardizing the opportunity.

Most times you will be given that, even expected to take it. You need the time to cooly measure the offer, to let the natural excitement of a new opportunity subside. Second thoughts are as important as first impressions here. If you aren't given time to mull things over, that may raise questions in itself about what kind of job you have been offered. It may be that the job is a real clunker that's hard to fill. They want you to say "yes" before you have time to learn that. Or maybe the company is struggling with a disaster and needs someone in the breech—only to concede the battle three or four months later and put you on the street.

When you look at any offer, you're measuring three factors: the company, the job, and salary and benefits.

The Company

Much of the corporate research you did as you began your search applies now. Review those materials and the conversations you've had with members of your network who have knowledge of the company that made the offer. Look again at profits and performance, checking in *Value Line* or *Standard & Poor's* for the latest figures. Is the company on the rise or stagnating? How about the industry? The competition—stronger or weaker? What's happening in the division where you would work? Success or failure? Is it the stepchild of the company or its star performer? Read current trade publications to update the corporation's image and what's being reported about it. You might learn of pending mergers that could mean big changes in the job you are considering. Or you may find the company has hit a legal snag that could tie up your division for years in litigation.

If you aren't given time to mull things over, that may raise questions in itself about what kind of job you've been offered.

What else does the company do? If it's a far-flung holding operation, you should know what's flung out there. You need to know the overall health of the company, its scope and where it's putting its resources. A string of acquisitions in food service would tell you where the money and attention are going. You'll also pinpoint other opportunities in the company, knowledge you may want to keep in the back of your head for future reference.

Face to face with corporate culture

Here, too, you can add another chapter to your corporate-culture research. Are you comfortable with how you have been treated and how the offices are designed? What provisions are there for the welfare of all employees, such as safe parking, an on-duty nurse or an acceptable cafeteria? Read the employee newsletter. Is it little more than a bulletin board or a genuine source of communication among all levels of the company?

Now is the time to question employees if you can. Ask to meet with people you will be working with. Sometimes you'll find this is part of the script anyway, and a parade of people will greet you either in the interview room or as you are taken around to their offices. Some companies control this process—the person in charge stays with you. Other companies, perhaps more confident of how they are perceived by their employees, let you talk alone with the employees.

Seek mid- and lower-level people. Ask them how one gets ahead, what life is like there.

"I'm sure you'll love working at the Branch Office That Time Forgot."

Toos, Cartoonists & Writers Syndicate

Ask how long they have worked at the company and what other jobs they may have held. You want to learn if there is promotion from within or transferring from one division to another. Once more, a company's reaction may say a lot; a disaffected employee a lot more. Or you may find the corporate line is true. The place is great.

If you talk with employees who recently joined the company, ask them if they've passed the rookie stage yet. Some companies consider lunch the cutoff point while others measure growth like annual rings on a tree, slowly and evenly.

As you talk, listen as much for what isn't said as what is. Of course, you've got to allow for an individual's personality, but note whether the conversation is cordial or stiff. Are you hearing measured, carefully rehearsed responses or spontaneous answers to your questions? Do you hear anything critical? No job is perfect, the criticism is perhaps more important as an indication of openness than as a comment on the workplace. But do consider what you hear.

Talk to ex-employees. They may be difficult to locate, but your network may provide some names, as will your research into the firm. You may ask for names during your negotiating. Judge the responses—both the company's to your request and what the former employees tell you—as part of your research. Bear in mind that you'll get a careful selection of names that will undoubtedly yield only positive assessments—unless, of course, the company wasn't listening to its people to begin with and didn't know just how unhappy some of them were. And that will also tell you something about the company.

After you've toted up the facts, ask yourself how this compares with what you have; with other offers you may be considering; with your short- and long-term goals.

The Position

Somehow, what is probably the most important part of an offer often gets the least scrutiny. It's common to look at a company ("great reputation") and the salary ("nice boost from what I was getting") and leave the position to evolve. Maybe that's ego—you think you'll mold it to your vision—or you see it as a foot in the door, a job you'll be moved up from in a little while.

Talk with the people you'll work with, with mid- to lower-level employees, and with ex-employees if possible.

continued on page 231

Larry King: Working Overseas

Each day Bloomberg News Service editor Larry King deals with incoming stories from 16 bureaus in Europe, Asia and Africa. His 12-hour days begin between six and six-thirty each morning. What makes the demanding work so interesting is that King is doing it in London.

Working overseas is a dream for many and a requirement for plenty of others who are to use time spent in important foreign operations to gild their rising careers. For King, who turned down the chance to work overseas early in his career at the financial news service, the shift from New York City to London came once he felt he knew enough about both financial reporting and Bloomberg, a relatively new but rapidly growing financial news service.

"Turning down the offer did not damage my career," says King. Instead, it allowed him to strengthen his chances for success. It's a lesson many potential overseas employees can benefit from.

"A lot of people view New York as the Mother Church and they worry more about what is going on there. If I hadn't worked there, I'd be paranoid, too, because of the isolation [of being so far from there].

"You don't understand the thinking, and who is making the decision. You just get things handed to you. You get phone calls and electronic mail and you don't understand them. But because I was there in New York, I understand the thinking, and who is making the decisions."

There's a balancing act involved in working in another culture, even one as seemingly friendly as England. "You have to come to grips with the fact that you are in a foreign country and you have to adapt to the way they do things," said King. At the same time, you have to make them understand that this is a company and things are not always going to be done the way they are in a foreign country. Balancing the two is the key to success."

Although he's single, King says another challenge facing many overseas workers is work for "trailing" spouses. Most times, there aren't any jobs because of language barriers, work rules or local customs. "There are a lot of husbands and wives undergoing enforced idleness in a foreign country where they may not be versed in the language and they're sitting home all day. That can be hard on a family."

King says there are organizations in most large cities that offer help for expatriates, especially trailing spouses, and the opportunity to meet and get to know one another and most employers with foreign operations can put their own workers in touch with them.

As for expenses in one of the world's most expensive cities, King says he's managed to make the move without hardship. His company adjusted his pay upward, and he scoured London until he found an affordable apartment in South Kensington where the rent matched what he had paid in New York City. He gets no breaks on taxes—expatriates pay the local levy. "It's not a problem because New York's taxes were high. But if I'd come from a cheaper place, it would have been an issue," he explains.

But it is what you will be doing for some period of time, and—unless you ignore it altogether or lie about it on your resume—it will become a permanent part of how you are judged in the marketplace, and you'll have to explain it to someone before you get another job somewhere else.

What will you be doing? It's surprising how vague some managers make a job description when they offer it verbally. That's why you should have an offer letter in hand before you decide. Such letters are common for middle managers and even high-level managers, although the latter generally require contracts that outline their compensation and severance packages in greater detail.

Once you have the letter, review it against the notes you made at the time the offer was made. How complete a description is it? Are your duties and responsibilities clearly and completely defined? Does it state to whom you will report and those who will report to you? Are all the salary, bonus and benefits you discussed in the interview outlined in detail here? How often will your performance be evaluated? What constitutes success on the job you are being offered? That may not be spelled out in the offer letter, but you should have a complete idea of what's expected of you.

How does the offer compare with both your short- and long-term goals? You may be willing to take it on the chin financially for a little while to get yourself established, especially if you are changing fields. Starting sales positions can pay relatively low wages, yet zoom once your contacts are in place and a few good contracts come in. The same can hold true for other professions, such as jobs in radio and television news, for example, where salaries in small cities are commensurate with the size but six-figure contracts at the network level are common.

If you're switching or dramatically changing the scope of your responsibilities, you must do more digging to be sure your path leads upward, not just outward, or in the worst circumstances, down. One company may see an entry- or lower-level position as an audition from which only a few will be chosen, the rest left to squander their time if they aren't smart enough to move on. Competitive big-city law firms often operate like that: "up or out" is the

Do some more digging to be sure your path leads upward, not just outward, or in the worst circumstances, down.

motto that applies to a career there. Yet, another kind of business may see its lower ranks as the seasoning pot for its next generation of leaders and regard anyone who made it inside the door as worthy of a long-time commitment from the company. Lands' End, the catalog clothing-retailer, prides itself on its drive to raise its own upper-echelon talent. Much of this has to do with the culture of the company you're considering, something you'll discover in your research and interviews.

Even if you're unemployed and feel desperate to return to work, consider the path you'll take with each offer you receive.

Salary and Benefits

There is a number on the table. Can you accept it? That's the bottom line to the, well, bottom line. You are, after all, in large part doing this for the money. If the process went as it should, the money and benefits are what you expected them to offer. But there's that hard figure.

- **Are you comfortable with it?**

- **How does it compare with others in your field who are doing the same work?**

- **How does it compare with your notion of what you should receive?**

- **Do the benefits equal what you have where you are now?** If not, and that's an issue, what will it cost to bring them into line?

- **What if the salary is much higher?** Be sure it's because you were underpaid, not because the company is desperate to fill an awful job.

- **What about bonuses?** Are they linked to performance? The company's? That's common today as firms move from across-the-board pay hikes to ones linked to action and gain. You can expect bonuses for middle managers to range from 5% to 20% annually. But bonuses are not as widespread as they used to be. Companies are rethinking who is important and who is not, and rewarding accordingly.

How do you measure other benefits?

You can compare health plans by what they cover. Basic conventional coverage takes care of about 80% of health care costs such as hospitalization and doctor visits. Comparing health costs will take some work on your part. Be sure to look at deductibles, co-payments and lifetime caps on benefits. Better HMO plans add dental, eye-care and psychiatric care. Premium

"We're facing a crisis, Holbrook.
They're breaking through the glass ceiling!"

Bart, Cartoonists & Writers Syndicate

plans add drug- and alcohol–abuse treatment and orthodontic care for you and your family. You may be offered a liberal leave policy for maternity (or even paternity). There may be a childcare program or payment for childcare. You may also be eligible to receive retirement and financial counseling at little or reduced cost. Many companies now offer what they call "cafeteria" plans to reduce costs. You pick among benefits only those you need.

You may find fitness and illness-prevention stressed with programs that pay for health club membership or provide for on-the-premises exercise programs. You may be offered stress reduction classes and blood pressure and cholesterol clinics as ways the company tries to keep its employees well.

Be certain you know whether the new health plan will cover any preexisting medical conditions you or your family may have.

Be sure you understand when coverage begins. You may need to extend your existing health insurance until you are covered.

Tuition reimbursement plans are increasingly common. Subsidized cafeterias, company-made product

Even after they are made, most offers have some give built into them, as much as 10% or 15%.

discounts and company travel packages that reduce the cost of your vacation are other ways companies add to the value of an offer.

Pension plans are yet another factor to consider, especially if you are older. Be certain you are being offered a pension. Many companies have abandoned them in favor of 401(k) plans. Under these plans, you contribute a portion of your income toward your pension. Your company may match that by a percentage. (Good plans offer 50% or more of your contribution as a match.) The money you give comes off the top of your income; you aren't taxed on it and you won't be until you withdraw it. To provide an incentive for you to keep the money for your retirement, the IRS assesses a 10% penalty on top of the income tax on each withdrawal before you reach 59½. These plans are more common in larger companies, but increasingly you'll find them in smaller firms. The plans are attractive in a key way—you take your cumulative earnings with you when you leave the company. Unless you're vested in a plan, you can't do that with a pension.

To compare pension plans you can ask for an estimate of what you would receive after ten or 20 years.

You should consider your age and health and any special needs you or your family might have when you judge benefits. For example, if your kids need braces, you'll be more interested in the company's orthodontic coverage than someone who is approaching retirement. Or, if you have plans to begin a graduate program, tuition reimbursement would have real value to you.

Negotiating

You know what you have, and you know what you want. There's an offer on the table but it isn't quite right. You can barter the major elements of an offer—salary, bonuses and perhaps benefits. But how much? And how? Even after they are made, most offers have some give built into them, as much as 10% or 15%, just so there can be some negotiation. Getting it, however, takes planning.

Most important may be timing.

You have a moment, a window of opportunity, in the time after the offer is made and before you accept, that is optimum. The company wants you but it doesn't have you yet. Goodwill is high; you have the advantage. Once you accept, your power to alter the terms of the contract pretty much vanishes. You risk alienating your new boss if you reopen negotiations. So preserve your position by not immediately accepting an offer.

As noted earlier, you can ask for up to a week to consider the offer.

This is especially so for higher-ranking jobs. Most initial offers are verbal ones. Take careful notes and review them so that you can compare them with a later offer letter. You may want to consult with those members of your network with knowledge of the company to see if what you are getting seems reasonable.

List what you like and what you don't like.

When they toss the ball in your court, it may have a wobble on it you didn't see before. It's easy in the reverie of company-matching-up-with-employee to miss something. Is the salary on the mark or a little low? Is the job description what you thought it would be or off a notch or two? You don't get marketing, after all. You're in the satellite building, not headquarters. To flip the coin, are there any tradeoffs that neutralize a negative? An extra week of vacation? A bigger stock option? A larger guaranteed bonus?

Make sure you still want this job.

Do you even want this job now that time has passed, you've considered the offer and the conditions of the job? This is mulling time, time when you talk it over with your spouse, your family, your colleagues and yourself.

In time a picture of what you want will evolve in your mind. Then you negotiate. Good negotiating leaves both sides feeling they won. Anything less, a loss-win situation

Taking a job you don't want can put you back where you started, unhappy and looking for work.

where you feel cheated or a win-lose situation where the company feels blackmailed, can breed resentment you'll have to deal with later.

For each counteroffer you make, have an explanation for why it would be justified.

You already get four weeks of vacation, not three; your current bonus plan is worth 50% of your salary, not just 25%; you will need a company car for the extra travel you will be doing. If salary is an issue, offer a range you would consider. Let it fall near the offer you have received but of course have it skew in your favor. For example, if you have been offered $45,000 and you want something closer to $50,000, you might say you were looking for something between $47,000 and $53,000. That gives the company some latitude and leaves you flexible, too. It's a mistake to take a rigid stance, saying you want $50,000 or no deal, especially if it's a job you want. Strong-arm tactics like that peg you as difficult. A company may decide to take advantage of the opportunity to end its dealings with you.

Know what you want, but bear in mind that good negotiating involves give and take.

Be willing to compromise on those items you don't consider deal-breakers. You may find it helpful to keep your strong points on the table, reviewing them with the company as you negotiate. Remind them of the significant amount of time you spend in the international marketing department where you are, perhaps an area the company would like to expand. Or review your record at cost cutting in shipping and receiving. Or point out that you can be on the job in under a month. Cite your research on salary and benefits in the industry (it's not as irritating to the company as reviewing what you have where you are). The point is, you have reasons for expecting more than what's being offered.

continued on page 238

Acceptance Letter

Dana P. Williams
2 Park Street
Martinsburg, MO 40513
305-555-1243

July 29, 1997

Jacob Henry, President
Compu-Card Corp.
19 Pine St.
West Palm Beach, FL 33408

Dear Mr. Henry:

This letter confirms my acceptance of your offer for the assistant director of informational systems as outlined in your letter dated July 21, 1997, which outlines salary and benefits.

As we agreed, I will assume my duties in the Boca Raton branch on August 20, 1997, but will be absent for the week of September 5-10 to oversee the moving of my family to Boca Raton.

It's been a pleasure getting to know you, Jacob, and the Compu-Card Corp. I look forward to working with you and your fine staff.

Sincerely,

Dana P. Williams

A letter carries as much legal weight as a contract but provides more protection if the deal goes sour: What's not in writing can be negotiated.

Even if it isn't so, maintain an inner attitude that you are happy where you are; you don't need *this* job.

Your dissatisfaction with your current job may be acute—you may be unemployed—but leaping to another job for no better reason than it is something else somewhere else is pointless. Sometimes it's far more than that. Taking a job you don't want can turn into a disaster, leave you with a black mark on your record and put you back where you started, unhappy and looking for work.

Saying Yes

Let's say, however, that you avoid those pitfalls. Your negotiations end successfully. You shake on the deal. Now what? You can accept an offer verbally, but get the details in writing before you give notice to your current boss. Review the written terms carefully against your notes and what you believed you were being offered. Like a final fitting for a custom suit, be sure this is what you thought you were getting. Honest misunderstandings here aren't seen in the same light as your reopening negotiations because you have changed your mind. Ask questions if you have any and be satisfied with the answers before you move.

Accept the offer in writing, making note of the terms outlined in the offer letter and any other arrangements you have made since then. Date the letter and include the date you will report to work. Send it to the person who made you the offer. You can find an example of an acceptance letter on page 237.

Do you need a contract? Or an attorney? Most often no. A letter carries as much legal weight as a contract but actually leaves you with more protection should the deal go sour. That's because what's not in writing can be negotiated. Implied contracts, customs, the way you were treated, can enter into the discussions if regrettably you get snagged up in the new job and either want out or are pushed out. Contracts, not common in middle management positions, tend to box you in and cut rights away from you.

While you may not need a contract for the main

offer, you will probably have documents attached, or provided at some point before you accept, that outline the provisions of stock options, pension plans or other deferred compensation. These are legal documents, and they amount to a contract so you should have an attorney review them before you sign anything or agree to accept the offer.

If you take the job, review how to leave a company as outlined in Chapter 2.

What if you really want to stay where you are, but you have a tempting offer? Circumstances vary, but as we noted earlier, bargaining with a job offer should be done only if you are willing to leave. You may be a valued employee and your company may make a generous counteroffer to keep you on board. You may find your boss willing to confess that you were underpaid or your skills were wasted on lower-level jobs. You may find yourself a notch or two higher on the organization chart, your prestige heightened. But again, you have, even if you were contacted rather than sought out the offer, signaled you are looking or willing to be courted. Bargaining with an offer from another company is seen by many as the crudest of tactics.

Of course that doesn't mean people don't leave and come back to their old jobs or a better one a few months or even a few years later. That's one more reason to part ways as amiably as you can with an old employer, even if you have been let go. You may live to work there another day.

If you say "no" to the offer, mind your manners there, too. Explain your reasons for not accepting, and make them reasonable. If circumstances change in the future, you may want to apply for work there again. Or they might have another, more favorable, position that would be perfect for you. And don't underestimate the value of another factor. You've probably added a number of people at the company to your network. After all, they liked you well enough to offer you a job.

Staying in Charge

This book began with your unhappiness and ends with tips on how to keep your new-found satisfaction in place. Along with your own acceptable performance and your company's delivery on all the promises it made, there remains the matter of fitting in. You may recall it as one of the questions that must be answered before you will get an offer. Now you have accepted that offer, you've come on board and you're working hard. But are you going to fit in? Everybody's got their fingers crossed. You have done your homework, but the studious observance of your company's culture does not end the day your stationery arrives. You face initiations of several stripes. Your loyalty is not proven, your attitude toward your colleagues remains to be assessed.

You may be more than just a new employee. You may be the boss, too. You've got a powerful challenge ahead of you for you will have to learn the language as well as teach it. Succeed and you and your new subordinates meld into culture you both can live with. Fail, and somebody's out the door.

Learning the language isn't the only challenge you face. Down the road you may be part of a merger or buyout where all, or most, of the rules get turned on their heads. Survival comes to those who quickly enroll in the new culture and speak the new tongue as fast as they can.

Fitting In

Your own expectations are as much conjecture as the result of your diligent research. You'll need the cooperation, even the hearty support of your fellow workers. They'll give it in dosages commensurate with your skills at understanding and respecting what they do.

It's a heady time, fraught with potential for both success and failure. And you barely know your way to the restroom.

So once you are on board, give yourself at least six months to get a sense of the place. Unless you are totally wrong for the job, this is a time you're entitled to some grace and a few mistakes. It may extend to a year or even 18 months in some organizations. Whatever the time period, it is your responsibility to find out how much of a honeymoon you will have. One way to protect your fledgling tenure is to turn to a veteran or two, relatively high in the organization but not at the top, for help. You want people who are knowledgeable, but not so powerful they must be too discreet.

"HIRED!"

Schwadron, Cartoonists & Writers Syndicate

Don't make your actions sound like a conspiracy. Be friendly, you're only seeking information to help you understand. When you have a question about how things are running, don't use names, if possible; instead refer to divisions or departments. Rather than, "Does North get along with Baker?" say, "Is the freight department aware of what international sales is doing?"

Observe the Junior Execs

An excellent gauge of a corporation's culture is its junior-level executives. As a guide to your own behavior, watch how they react in any situation with senior management. Do they lay back waiting for the latter to take a position before they act? Or do they enter an ongoing discussion, offering their opinions as their boss does? Once a position is known, do they challenge it? At management meetings, pay attention to the tone of reports. If they are all positive, you know people are reluctant to say what's on their minds. Honest discussion is taking place elsewhere, either in offices or over lunch somewhere.

If you move to a small company, you'll obviously have fewer choices and probably a lot less time in which to figure out where the skeletons are buried. On the other hand, you'll be stepping into a smaller bureaucracy and be given more latitude as a result. Either way you'll find some practices and values universal.

Watch the Rituals

Assign values to them. In some companies you'll miss a staff meeting only if you consider your days there numbered. In other places your absence denotes your workload and is only regretted. Play ball? Sometimes you'd better. If you're in a "work hard, play hard" culture, the company team is required duty.

Beyond physical fitness, it's one more way the company says you're a part of a team of people who like competition and are used to winning. Unsaid in all the rah-rah is that team effort counts more than your individual contribution.

Then there are places that are little more than bunkhouses for the cowboys who work there. These people are all swash and buckle, landing big deals, celebrating heartily every time the company makes another million in fees. You might even see a dinner bell hanging in a prominent location near the central gathering place, ready to be rung every time the company wins another contract. Friday afternoon beer busts are as close as anyone here gets to a staff meeting. You'll fit in with a flashier wardrobe, and as much lore about yourself as you can generate, be it the size of your expense vouchers or

continued on page 244

Phyllis Hoffman: Shifting to a Small Company

Phyllis Hoffman thought she was a lifer at Dun & Bradstreet outside of Philadelphia. Then the ax fell on her 14-year career as vice president of internal communications for two divisions of the big data and research firm.

The reorganization that cost Hoffman her job left her with feelings typical of loyal employees: "The most painful part was wondering, how could I have worked there so long and now they can [do] without me?" Hunting high and low for a new job, she acted on a tip from a company vendor and a corporate headhunter that a nearby firm was looking for a communications professional.

The tip paid off, and in a matter of months Hoffman was named vice president of corporate communications for Advanta Corp., a financial services company just five miles from her old job. "I'd never heard of them," she admits.

It's no wonder. Where her unit of Dun & Bradstreet employed 25,000 in 90 countries, Advanta did business with just a tenth the number of workers. There were plenty of other differences, too, that made the shift from a large corporation to a smaller one extremely challenging.

While many of the actual job responsibilities are the same as in her old position, says Hoffman (such as handling advertising, marketing and employee communications), "everything moves at a faster pace."

"There are fewer layers and less bureaucracy so that it's almost frenetic. You don't have to wait for a decision. Time lines for projects are very condensed. At Dun & Bradstreet, time lines gradually eroded away over time as the company got bigger and bigger."

Does Hoffman like the difference? For the most part. "I have a sense that I can make a real difference. You would think that with a 25,000-person audience (at Dun & Bradstreet) you would have a greater impact. But the impact is watered down. Here, you can work from scratch, and that is more fun than maintaining or overhauling a big company."

Big companies are known for their pay and benefits, too. Hoffman took a slight pay cut to join Advanta; she doesn't know how long it will take to make it up. There's no pension plan at the company but employees can buy shares at a reduced rate in a stock option plan. The company has a 401(k) plan, though she stayed in her old plan because she missed the open period when the company allowed new enrollees to join.

Hoffman also stayed on her old company's health insurance plan while she was between jobs. She locked in for a year, so she ended up paying for it out of her own pocket at the same time she was purchasing coverage from Advanta. If she had waited until her interim coverage expired before joining Advanta's plan, she'd have needed to have a physical, and she felt it was just simpler to pay for both for the time being.

"I think I'm going to be much happier day to day here," she says. The specter of job insecurity that the Dun & Bradstreet layoff prompted does not easily go away. "This is a healthy business with good long-term prospects. This may be a short term trade-off on pay, but I'll be better off in the long run."

Gilt by association is an attribute of the first magnitude.

the number of days that have passed since anyone last saw you in the office.

What Determines Success?

You may find that the quarterly report rules where you are, while at another place it is market share. Or it may be quality, the buzzword of the '90s, which gets linked with customer satisfaction and employee entrepreneurship into an amalgam corporate leaders hope translates into more profits and a bigger market share. Some companies mean it when they insist they will market nothing that is not the best that can be made. These are all very different approaches to doing the same business. Or maybe it is the process that dominates, not the product. Breakfast cereal, within the limits of taste and hygiene, is not going to demand high quality. Process is everything as 10 tons of mushy wheat germ begins its journey through a block-long oven. There had better be an empty box waiting at the other end.

You can see how disastrous the wrong approach could be in each place.

Get to Know the "Heroes"

You know who's in charge. How about the heroes? Make a list of the people in your company who have the respect or influence that would rank them as heroes. Anyone can be on the list, from the head of building maintenance (the guy who kept the computers cool during a heat wave) to the top sales person in the Midwest office who keeps flying back to give training sessions. These people hold symbolic power as well as any real power by virtue of how they are perceived. Make yourself known to them. Gilt by association is an attribute of the first magnitude.

Tap Into the Company Grapevine

Every company has one. Beyond your own group of lunch partners, you should attempt to "cross pollinate" with other groups or at least have contact with those with intra-group passage rights. Knowledge of shakeups in other departments can have meaning for you and the position you hold. They can signal tighter budgets or impending layoffs.

Adapt and Conquer

While you were wise to avoid a corporate culture you knew wouldn't fit your style, you're still going to find people within your new organization whose style won't jibe with yours. Fitting in means adapting to those differences even when the overall organization is more like you than the other person. Your goal is to be effective with as many people as you can. Often, simply being aware of your style can help you navigate through other "sub" cultures in your company. And that's the goal of fitting in.

For example, if your style is what would be broadly labeled as people-oriented, you might have a hard time commanding the attention of someone who's essentially a bottom-line personality. If you start a presentation with how a proposed cost-cutting program will adversely effect employee morale, you may find an unsympathetic ear. Begin instead by pointing out that, while the proposal will save money, it also will probably result in a loss of productivity among disgruntled workers—thus reducing the savings. Now you've got your boss's attention and you can offer your alternative, which, while reducing costs by a smaller amount will also be less likely to reduce employee dissatisfaction. With your idea, the company will save the same amount without hurting its employees.

Surviving Merger Culture

Even if you don't move to a different company, you may find a new company thrust upon you in the form

Simply being aware of your style can help you navigate through other "sub" cultures in your company.

continued on page 247

If You're the New Boss

You may find yourself in a coveted corner office with three windows. You're not just fitting in, you're in charge. You're new. Everyone else has questions for you. You hadn't given that much thought.

Below are 30 questions your employees are likely to have in mind. They are enlightening. Try answering them in your own situation. Even if you're not the boss—yet—the questions raise interesting issues about how differently a boss and an employee can do business and how critical knowing preferences can be.

- What do you expect of me?

- What are your productivity goals?

- What is your definition of a top performer?

- How do you measure productivity?

- How will I know if my performance displeases you?

- How receptive are you to productivity innovations?

- Are you willing to take risks and to what degree?

- How far down do you intend to push the decision-making process?

- What should I do if I think you are making a mistake?

- Do you have a negotiation period after you make a decision?

- If so, how should I approach you?

- How can I tell if something is important to you?

- How often do you want updates?

- How do you express your satisfaction?

- How do you handle conflict?

- What should I do if you lose your temper?

- Do you have any idiosyncrasies that I should know about?

- What are the ground rules for calling you at home?

- What are your strong points and weak points?

- Do you have strong feelings about any moral or ethical issues?

- What should I do if I feel my work puts me in an ethical bind?

- Do you accept rough drafts, or should everything be in final form?

- Do you expect written status reports?

- How do you send "zingers" to the staff?

- How much do you want to know about a problem?

- When do you prefer to get information?

- What is your number one priority in the next six months?

- What are your personal career goals?

- How much social interaction do you want me to have with you?

- How should I address you?

of one of the increasingly common corporate mergers and takeovers. Fitting in to this new arrangement requires some different considerations.

Welcome to hard times. Only massive layoffs or plant closings can shake up a company more than a merger, especially if your side is seen as the one being taken over. A 1991 study by Robert Half International, the California-based executive recruiter, found that for nearly half of the executives it polled, getting caught up in a merger was the greatest fear they had. (Being fired was their second greatest fear, while 12% put burn-out at the top of their list.)

Smoke screens go up when merger talk gets serious. Trusted lines of cross-corporate communication may be destroyed overnight as people clam up in an effort to protect their positions. Energy once devoted to the job gets channeled into the trenches as the warfare begins.

Henry Ryan, whom you met in Chapter 2 when he was part of the Gulf-Chevron merger, found himself on the vanquished side of the deal, despite Chevron's attempts to make it seem like a true melding of equal partners.

"They were very humane trying to assimilate the people," he said of his brief stay in San Francisco, where Chevron is headquartered. "But obviously, they were able to buy us, not the other way around."

If Ryan's experience is typical, the fear that even merger talk engenders is often justified.

"There's no merger without hardship," he says, remembering several colleagues still looking for work five years later. "I don't know if anyone benefits except the shareholders [whose investment may rise dramatically in a sweetened purchase offer].

"When I went to Gulf Oil I thought it would be the last company I worked for. I was prepared to retire from there. What it pointed out to me was the uncertainty of life. That really changed me."

Don't automatically view the buyer as the enemy. A new partner may bring infusions of cash, opportunities and fresh energy.

Mergers Can Mean Opportunity

"Guess who got promoted to a desk with no drawers?"

From the Wall Street Journal, Permission,
Cartoon Features Syndicate

That uncertainty is born of change, but change isn't always negative. If you're in the company being acquired, don't automatically view the buyer as the enemy. While the story of mergers is often one of downsizing, a new partner may bring infusions of cash, opportunities and fresh energy. Old lines of management that may have hampered your career could change. If your division was a rose in a garden of cash-draining thorns, you may find your status on the rise. Or it may be that clearing the decks of the old ways is just the boost you need for a second wind with the company.

That's not to say there aren't risks, especially if the firm acquiring yours is in the same business and thus staffed with people who have your skills or experience.

You can begin opening lines of communication by contacting anyone you have identified as your counterpart in the other company. Be careful to keep within your strata, or your efforts may be misinterpreted as threatening to your boss.

Even if the company buying your firm has better manners, just melding operations is tough. You may find that your people were faster at making decisions, but behind in technology to implement them. That's a common condition, not limited to mergers. Consider your own firm's various components. Most companies are challenged by the rigors of keeping all departments humming along at the same speed.

You may find the new culture jarring, and you're entitled not to like what's happening. You've been shaken out of your routine, your network turned upside down. But give it six months before you make any decisions about whether the merger is working for you. In that time you may discover the merger brought you new opportunity.

The bad times are over. You've taken charge, now you should plan to stay in charge.

Staying Fit

So you're in. This job is going to work. The bad times are a fading memory. While you're entitled to the laurels of a new-found position, the last thing you should be doing now is resting on them. You've taken charge, now you should plan to stay in charge.

Like the dieter who has reached an ideal weight, now you're on a maintenance program, keeping up with trade journals, lunching with members of your network, researching your competition so you know what's out there. You're keeping track of your company's performance, how your division did last quarter, how the field looks in the year ahead. You know your chances for a promotion, you understand why you got the bonus you did last year. You're exercising regularly, keeping your outside interests up and controlling the stress in your work.

You've enrolled in a computer course, and you're practicing your Spanish so you won't get rusty. You're plugged into the interoffice network, so you know what's going on upstairs in the boardroom. You updated your resume just last month.

If you've spotted some troublesome signs on the horizon you're doing informational interviews to keep track of opportunities in other companies. You're being careful, however, and doing it on your own time.

In short, you're doing almost everything outlined in this book to *take* charge of your career, only now it is to *stay* in charge. You know from experience that career planning is not something you do only when calamity strikes but something you do every day you work.